CULTURES OF THE WORLD®

TANZANIA

Jay Heale & Winnie Wong

 Marshall Cavendish
Benchmark

New York

PICTURE CREDITS

Cover photo: © Sean Sprague / The Image Works

alt.TYPE / REUTERS: 33, 118 • Bjorn Klingwall: 39 • Corbis: 24, 30, 45, 55, 57, 72, 96, 126, 127 • Dave G. Houser: 35 • Focus Team Italy: 7, 9, 16, 91, 106 • Francis Tan: 131 • Getty Images: 36, 37, 38, 48, 54, 67, 75, 93, 110 • Hoa-Qui: 74, 97, 101, 113, 121 • Hutchison Library: 29, 44, 63, 89, 100 • Images of Africa Photobank: 3, 10, 17, 59, 62, 70, 73, 95, 107 • Jason Laure: 14 • Liba Taylor: 21, 71, 90 • Lonely Planet Images: 1, 4, 5, 27, 28, 43, 50, 52, 53, 58, 60, 61, 64, 68, 78, 80, 86, 87, 92, 94, 98, 104, 105, 122, 123, 129 • National Geographic: 6, 18, 41, 42, 47, 49, 65, 77, 111, 120 • North Wind Picture Archives: 23, 25 • Photolibrary: 8, 11, 12, 19, 20, 32, 56, 66, 69, 79, 82, 83, 88, 102, 103, 108, 112, 130 • Robert Pateman: 34 • Still Pictures: 15, 46, 125, 128 • Sue Cunningham Photography: 84, 119 • Sylvia Cordaly Photo Library Ltd: 13 • TopFoto: 81 • TRIP Photographic Library: 114, 116, 117

PRECEDING PAGE

A group of school children sitting by a wall.

Publisher (U.S.): Michelle Bisson
Editors: Deborah Grahame, Mindy Pang
Copyreader: Tara Koellhoffer
Designer: Geoslyn Lim
Cover picture researcher: Connie Gardner
Picture researcher: Thomas Khoo

Marshall Cavendish Benchmark
99 White Plains Road
Tarrytown, NY 10591
Website: www.marshallcavendish.us

Originated and designed by Times Media Private Limited
An imprint of Marshall Cavendish International (Asia) Private Limited
A member of Times Publishing Limited

Marshall Cavendish is a trademark of Times Publishing Limited.

Library of Congress Cataloging-in-Publication Data
Heale, Jay.
  Tanzania / by Jay Heale & Winnie Wong. — 2nd ed.
    p. cm. — (Cultures of the world)
  Summary: "Provides comprehensive information on the geography, history, wildlife, governmental structure, economy, cultural diversity, peoples, religion, and culture of Tanzania"—Provided by publisher.
  Includes bibliographical references and index.
  ISBN 978-0-7614-3417-7
  1. Tanzania—Juvenile literature. I. Wong, Winnie. II. Title.
  DT438.H34 2009
  967.8—dc22   2008028802

Printed in China
7 6 5 4 3 2 1

CONTENTS

A Masai child holding a goat.

A traditional dhow off the coast of northern Zanzibar.

INTRODUCTION

TANZANIA IS HOME to a fascinating collection of wildlife, which is captured in eye-catching *tingatinga* (Tin-ga tin-ga) art or observed close-up in a safari. Natives grow their subsistence crops on sunbaked plains, around lakes, and on the slopes of snowcapped equatorial mountains. With a history that reaches back to prehistoric time, Tanzania is a melting pot of traditions, a crossroad of cultures, and a country of varied and unique people such as Masai warriors, Makonde sculptors, and Gogo musicians. Traders came to Tanzania for spices, slaves, and territory. The story of Tanzania is about a fight for freedom from slavery and colonial rule, and then for economic survival. Although their country is still poor, Tanzanians remain optimistic about their future as they combat drought, ill health, and food shortages to create a better environment for themselves and future generations.

GEOGRAPHY

TANZANIA IS THE LARGEST country in East Africa, covering 364,900 square miles (945,087 square km), including the offshore islands of Zanzibar, Pemba, and Mafia. It is bigger than Kenya and Uganda put together, and half as large again as Texas. It is bordered by eight countries: Kenya and Uganda to the north; Rwanda, Burundi, and Zaire to the west; and Zambia, Malawi, and Mozambique to the south. To the east lies the Indian Ocean.

Most of Tanzania is made up of high, hot plateau land that is over 600 feet (200 m) above sea level. Tanzania has the Indian Ocean to the east and the plunging line of rift valley lakes to the west, with more rift valley depressions through the center. The country's terrain includes the highest mountain in Africa, Mount Kilimanjaro, and the world's second-deepest lake, Lake Tanganyika. As with many African countries, Tanzania's ability to produce food is dwindling steadily. Much of what was once savannah and scattered bush is now turning into semidesert. Still it is home to a spectacular array of wildlife.

Left: **Wide savannah plains have only a few, scattered acacia trees.**

Opposite: **A beautiful coastal estuary at Pemba Island in Tanzania.**

The Olduvai Gorge is one portion of the rift valley stretch found in Tanzania.

RIFT VALLEYS

The Great Rift Valley is an important geological feature in East Africa. It is made up of a series of fault lines caused by volcanic activity. It stretches over 4,000 miles (6,500 km) and averages 30–40 miles (48–64 km) in width. The gigantic tear runs from Syria and the Jordan Valley in the north to Beira (Mozambique) in the south. Water has filled in some of the depressions, creating a series of deep lakes with floors well below sea level and surfaces several hundred meters above sea level. There are two rift valley branches in Tanzania: the western branch, which includes Lakes Tanganyika and Malawi, and the eastern branch, which extends all through Kenya to Lakes Natron and Eyasi and beyond.

LAKE TANGANYIKA, a rift valley lake, is the world's longest freshwater lake (420 miles/680 km), and it is so deep (4,710 feet/1,435 m) that it contains seven times the amount of water in Lake Victoria. Covering about 12,700 square miles (32,900 square km), Lake Tanganyika forms the boundary between Tanzania and the Democratic Republic of Congo. It is

There are old African stories about a great flood that swallowed up plains that were once rich in cattle. These stories may well refer to the way that rift lakes, such as Lake Tanganyika, were formed.

home to more than 250 species of fish, several species of crab, and the eastern aquatic cobra, a unique snake that eats fish in the lake and relaxes on the rocks of the shore under the warm sun. Hippopotami and crocodiles abound in the lake's brackish waters.

LAKE VICTORIA

The northwest corner of Tanzania is occupied by a large part of Lake Victoria, which Tanzania shares with Uganda and Kenya. More like an inland sea, Lake Victoria is so large that it has its own local climate (usually cloudy and humid). It is almost 27,000 square miles (69,484 square km) in area. Its southern waters provide Tanzania with fresh fish, a ferry route to Uganda, numerous small islands, and an extensive, fertile shoreline that is dotted with fields of tea, coffee, and cotton crops. Rapidly spreading hyacinth weed has become a problem in some areas of the lake. The dense weed blocks sunlight, which causes many fish to die. Dangerous creatures, including snakes and crocodiles, lurk underneath the hyacinth weed's heavily branched, fibrous root system. Yet Lake Victoria continues to provide one of the largest catches of fish in Africa.

The fishermen who live on the shore of Lake Tanganyika attract small dagaa fish on moonless nights using lights suspended from their boats.

RIVERS

The major rivers of Tanzania are the Rufiji, the Ruvuma, the Wami, and the Pangani. All these rivers drain into the Indian Ocean. Rufiji River is one of the great rivers of Africa. Wide and dangerous at flood time, it loops its way toward the sea, where it becomes choked by mangrove forests. Other minor rivers drain into the Rift Valley basins.

To the Luo people of Kenya, Lake Victoria is known as Nam Lolwe, *which means "lake without end."*

VOLCANOES AND MOUNTAINS

The volcanic force that formed the rift valleys is still alive today; there are many active or semiactive volcanoes in the area. At 19,340 feet (5,895 m), Mount Kilimanjaro, once an active volcano, is the highest point in Africa. The mountain rises majestically from the plains to its snowcapped peaks. The southeastern slopes receive considerable amounts of rain and are very fertile. The Chaga people, who live on the fertile southern slopes of Mount Kilimanjaro, grow a variety of crops—in particular, coffee, which grows very well in the volcanic soils. The mountain is also popular with climbers and has drawn many tourists to Tanzania. The higher of the two peaks, Kibo, is now named Uhuru (Freedom) Point.

The huge Ngorongoro Crater is part of the mountain chain. This chain includes Ol Doinyo Lengai. It is the world's largest caldera or volcanic depression, which encloses an area of 100 square miles (260 square km). The Masai regularly graze their cattle there.

Ol Doinyo Lengai, towering 9,650 feet (2,878 m) to the west of Kilimanjaro, is still an active volcano. The native Masai people call it "Mountain of God." It pours out spurts of black lava that turn white within two days because contact with moisture in the air converts most of it to crystals of sodium carbonate, commonly known as washing soda, a crystalline form of sodium carbonate used for cleaning. Many of the surrounding lakes have high amounts of soda as a result. An eruption in 1966 shot a column of gas and cinders 5,000 feet (1,500 m) into the air. On March 30, 2006, some 3,000 people had to be evacuated from nearby villages when the Ol Doinyo Lengai erupted.

Ol Doinyo Lengai is known as the Mountain of God to the Masai.

THE PEAKS OF MOUNT KILIMANJARO

Mount Kilimanjaro (known affectionately as *Kili*) has two peaks, Kibo and Mawenzi. Their names, in the Chaga language, describe their appearance: The first means "spotted," and the second means "having a broken top." According to a Chaga legend, there were once two sisters, Mawenzi and Kibo, who were both the same height. However, Mawenzi was lazier than her sister Kibo, and used to take Kibo's food to avoid having to cook for herself. Kibo finally became angry one day and beat Mawenzi on the head with her wooden ladle. According to the Chaga, this is why the sister peak is lower and has bumps on its head!

Mount Meru, at 14,980 feet (4,564 m), is the second-highest mountain in Tanzania. It last erupted about a century ago. Nearly 400 species of birds and diverse wildlife, including leopards, now live in its forest. Both Mount Kilimanjaro and Mount Meru are part of the northern chain of mountains known as the Pare and Usumbara ranges, which extend from the northern coast in a southeast-to-northwest direction. Mountains in southern Tanzania include the Livingstone Mountains as well as Rungwe Mountain.

As wide as all the world, great, high and unbelievably white in the sun.

—*Ernest Hemingway, on Mount Kilimanjaro*

A view of the Indian Ocean at a beach on the island of Zanzibar.

THE CENTRAL PLATEAU

The only word to describe the central and western plains of Tanzania is *vast*. They cover more than one-third of the country and are hot, baked dry, fairly flat, and, in places, more vast and barren than words or pictures can convey. They are grassland country (savannah), with scattered thorny trees. In the dry season they can be close to semidesert.

EASTERN COAST

Nearly all of the eastern mainland coastline has unspoiled, white-sanded, palm-shaded beaches bordered by warm turquoise waters. The sea is teeming with marine life, at least where the reefs have not been destroyed by dynamite fishing.

Zanzibar Island (Unguja) and Pemba are two islands that lie off the coast of Tanzania's mainland. They are made of coralline rock and are

TSETSE FLY

Tsetse is the name for bloodsucking insects (*Glossina morsitans*) that are found mainly in central African countries. Their bite transmits a disease called sleeping sickness, which affects both humans and livestock animals such as cattle, horses, and goats. Many of the miombo woodland areas in southern, central, and western Tanzania are infested with tsetse flies. As a result they are very thinly populated by humans. In the 1990s Tanzania succeeded in eradicating the dreaded tsetse fly population from Zanzibar, located in eastern Tanzania, using a method known as Sterile Insect Technique (SIT). In SIT, radioactive rays are used to make the male fly sterile and unable to reproduce.

mostly low-lying. Zanzibar Island is 53 miles (85 km) long and 27 miles (43 km) wide. It has many clove and other spice plantations and groves of coconut palms.

CLIMATE

Tanzania has three main climatic zones: the hot, humid coastal strip; the dry central plateau; and the semi-temperate mountains. Along the coast (as well as near Lakes Malawi and Tanganyika) the climate is humid for most of the year, day and night, and the humidity is relieved only by sea breezes. On the higher inland plains it is hot and dry, but much cooler at night. In most of the highlands it is warm during the day and cold at night.

The varied topography of Tanzania results in an unpredictable climate and rainy seasons that vary in length and intensity in the different parts of the country.

The baobab tree is unmistakable with its enormous trunk, which can grow to 30 feet (9 m) in diameter. Baobab trees are pollinated by bats and live up to 2,000 years.

The equator crosses midway through Kenya, to the north of Tanzania. This means that it is hot year-round, with hardly any difference between summer and winter. About half of Tanzania receives less than 30 inches (76.2 cm) of rain each year and is thus arid or semiarid.

The central plateau gets under 40 inches (101.6 cm) of rainfall per year during the rainy season between December and May, and loses much of this through evaporation caused by the continual heat. On the coast rainfall is heavier. Nearly all of the precious rainfall happens between March and May. This rainfall is known as the long rain. There are lighter "short rains" that take place during November and December.

FLORA

The plant life of Tanzania varies from coconut palms and mangroves on the coast to the flat-topped thorn trees of the inland plains. The two main types of tree cover in Tanzania are the dry miombo woodlands, which consist of a sparse cover of deciduous trees with a few baobab trees in the south and west regions, and montane (typical mountain forest) on the foothills of the northern mountains where there is more rainfall. On the savannah plains there are only occasional thorny acacia varieties,

POACHING

The desire for conservation has been accompanied by the awareness that tourists will pay good money to view wildlife reserves. Unfortunately the establishment of reserves has meant that the surrounding human populations have been deprived of their hunting grounds. With a growing population there is an increasing need for food. Poaching to get elephant ivory and rhino horn became a significant problem when markets for these items started to grow. Tanzania is home to one of the largest remaining elephant populations in the world. Most of these elephants are found in the Selous Game Reserve. Around 20,000 elephants were killed for their ivory in only a couple of years during the 1980s. Elephant poaching continues to be a big problem today.

In the 20th century the black rhino population was reduced severely from several hundred thousand at the beginning of the century to a historic low of 2,410 in 1995. Efforts to protect this endangered species helped increase the numbers to 3,610 by 2003.

including the larger yellow-fever tree, which often grows near water. Figs and tamarinds sprout along the watercourses. After the rains flowers sprout quickly, including different varieties of African violets.

FAUNA

Tanzania has more than 310 species of mammals. About 10 percent of these are endangered, while 14 percent are endemic, specific to the environment of Tanzania. They include the wildebeest, zebra, giraffe, elephant, rhino, lion, and leopard. On riverbanks and lakeshores, crocodiles and hippopotami are common. Dugong and giant turtles live off the coast. There are more than a thousand bird species in Tanzania, including vultures—nature's cleaning crew, which clear the plains of animal corpses that would otherwise rot. Many of the animals are protected, either through the many designated wildlife parks or through specific measures against the poaching of animals such as rhinos and elephants.

Gombe Stream National Park is a famous chimpanzee sanctuary that is also known for the research that was done there by Dr. Jane Goodall. It is still one of the best places in the world to see wild chimpanzees in their natural habitat.

NATIONAL PARKS

Almost one-quarter of Tanzania's countryside has been designated as protected wildlife areas. The role of some 14 national parks is to preserve the country's rich natural heritage and to provide secure breeding grounds for its fauna and flora. At Ngorongoro and Serengeti, the annual migration involves more than 2 million animals. There are also smaller sanctuaries, such as Gombe Stream National Park, Ruaha National Park, Rungwa Reserve, and Manyara National Park.

SERENGETI NATIONAL PARK

Serengeti National Park is Tanzania's oldest and most popular park. It covers an area of 5,700 square miles (14,763 sq km). This park, which is linked with the Masai Mara Game Reserve in neighboring Kenya, has well over 1.7 million wildebeests, and close to a million other animals, including some 300,000 zebra and thousands of giraffes, elephants, lions, and different species of antelope. An area about the size of Connecticut was set aside in 1940, with the intention of preserving the already rapidly disappearing wildlife. The park's landscape varies from extensive grassland plains to savannah to more wooded areas in the west. Serengeti is famous for the annual 497-mile (800-km) migration in which herds of wildebeests, zebras, and Thomson gazelle begin the largest mammalian migration on Earth.

NGORONGORO CONSERVATION AREA

This popular reserve contains a nearly circular volcanic crater that measures 12.4 miles (20 km) across and is surrounded by rock walls some 2,000 feet (600 m) high. Contained within this World Heritage site, the animals live wild—elephants and elands, hyenas and zebras, leopards, cheetahs, and lions, and even a few carefully monitored black rhinos. Ostriches and crowned cranes stalk over the grassland, and the waters of Lake Magadi are often covered with pink flamingos.

SELOUS GAME RESERVE

Claiming to be the world's largest game reserve, Tanzanians point out that the Selous (se-LOO) covers 17,400 square miles (45,000 square km) of virtually untouched land in southeastern Tanzania. The magnificent Rufiji River loops its way through the area. Only the northern tip of the reserve has been explored, and even the rangers can only give wild guesses on how many thousands of elephants, wildebeests, buffalos, antelopes, or hippos the reserve contains.

SERENGETI MIGRATION

The northern part of Tanzania is one of the remaining areas of Africa in which a natural annual migration of animals takes place. During the early months of the year, half a million wildebeest calves are born on the rich volcanic plains around the Ngorongoro Crater. When the dry season starts in June, the grass dies and most animals migrate north to the Serengeti National Park, where it is wetter and tall savannah grasslands grow. Some 200,000 zebra lead the way, cropping the coarse tops of the long grass. As many as 1.5 million wildebeests follow, feeding on the exposed succulent leaves and cropping the grass short, but leaving enough for the Thomson's gazelles that follow to eat. More than 2.5 million animals in all make the trip. Their urge to migrate is so strong that the herds will swim across rivers, becoming easy prey for crocodiles that live in the water and for the many carnivores (lions, cheetahs, leopards, wild dogs, hyenas, and jackals) that live on land. By September the herds are usually 500 miles (800 km) to the north of the country, feeding in the Masai Mara Game Reserve (inside the border of Kenya). When the rainy season starts in December, the herds head south to areas where the nutritious new grass will provide grazing for the next year's calves.

Animals know no borders—the wildebeests migrate annually from Ngorongoro Crater and Serengeti National Park in Tanzania to the adjoining Masai Mara Game Reserve in Kenya.

An aerial view of Zanzibar's cultural center, Stone Town. Much of this city is a maze of twisting, narrow streets and buildings built of coral stone, which are still preserved to this day.

CITIES

Most Tanzanians live in rural areas, with only about one-third of the population living in the cities. Of these, almost 4 million reside in the capital city of Dar es Salaam on a quiet bay off the Indian Ocean coast. It is the entry point to the rest of Tanzania, whether one is traveling by road, rail, or air. *Dar*, as locals call it, was not a particularly picturesque city before the Germans colonized it in 1894. Due to massive immigration from rural areas, over 70 percent of Dar's population still lives in slums. The city had poor water, electricity, and sewage services. The outer perimeters of Dar es Salaam were no more attractive than those of other major African cities: There was a sprinkling of industrial works mixed with suburbs made up of shanty-lined alleys. Lines of laundry hung from the balconies of dusty tenement blocks. Today the once chaotic city is a vibrant and well-managed hub that runs on private-public partnerships. Through programs such as Sustainable Cities and Managing Water for African Cities, Tanzania and other African countries are expected to get rid

of their image as part of a rural continent. The Sustainable Cities project in Dar es Salaam was so successful that it is now being implemented in all Tanzanian cities and towns.

In 1862 Sultan Majid of Zanzibar founded a fishing village farther south of Zanzibar, on the mainland, with a natural harbor. He encouraged its use as a trading center. Four years later he built himself a "haven of peace," Dar es Salaam, a coral palace where he hoped to relax and get away from the worries of his troubled reign on Zanzibar. The place deserved its name. Some 30 years later it became the capital of German East Africa. It was regarded as the capital until 1973, when the seat of government was transferred to Dodoma. Dodoma is located in central Tanzania, and is also the capital of the Dodoma Region. It is the legislative capital of Tanzania, and the designated future national capital. The National Assembly meets in Dodoma on a regular basis.

Zanzibar Island (Unguja) lies just 22 miles (35 km) off the eastern coast of Tanzania. It has its own history and culture and, in many ways, it is independent of the mainland. Most of the population living there is Muslim.

Overlooking the Indian Ocean is the House of Wonders and the People's Palace, each of which was, at different times, the official residence of the Sultan of Zanzibar between 1880 and 1964.

HISTORY

TANZANIA HOLDS THE KEY to the beginnings of humankind. At Olduvai Gorge, on the edge of the Serengeti, the famous scientists Louis and Mary Leakey discovered the remains of humanlike creatures that were nearly 2 million years old. Louis Leakey gave his first find, *Homo habilis*, the nickname "Handy Man," because the evidence showed this man to be the earliest known to have used tools. Later Mary Leakey found 3.6-million-year-old footprints, which proved that these prehistoric humans had walked upright.

Little is known about the early residents of Tanzania, though they were probably hunters and gatherers. By about 3,000 years ago the land was peopled by herders from the Ethiopian region and by Bantu speakers of West African origin. These early herders evolved a system of local chieftainships and councils. In the central highlands they continued their customs in spite of the growing influence of immigrants along the coast.

Above: **A building in Old Stone Town in Zanzibar. Zanzibar's economic power was once so great that it was said "When the flute is played in Zanzibar, they dance at the lakes."**

Opposite: **An old Arab fortress found in Zanzibar. The fort was built around the 18th century by Omani Arabs as a defense against the Portuguese.**

Tanzania's more recent history has been primarily one of trade. The Phoenicians explored the eastern coast of Africa as early as 600 B.C. It seems likely that they came to Tanzania. Certainly the Romans knew about Kilimanjaro—the highest mountain in Africa, located in northeastern Tanzania, near the border with Kenya—and the Great Lakes that are located in eastern Africa. The coast had trading contacts with Arabia since the first century A.D., and by A.D. 800, many had settled on the coasts of Tanzania. Later the area attracted the attention of the Portuguese, and then the Germans and British, who became the colonial rulers of Tanzania. Independent since 1961, the country has struggled to overcome its economic problems.

The large quantity of Chinese pottery fragments discovered indicates that Pangani, on the eastern coast, must have had trade links with the Far East.

TRADERS ARRIVE

Traders in small boats were coming across the Indian Ocean as early as the first century A.D., and they became regular visitors to the eastern coast of Tanzania around A.D. 800. They came from Arabia, Persia, and India and settled in the coastal areas. They called Tanzania the Land of *Zinj*, meaning "Land of Blacks." These traders were joined around 400 years later by the Shirazis (who originally came from Persia). Many married the local Africans. This was the beginning of the Swahili people. Their language, Kiswahili, would eventually be spoken throughout East Africa.

THE COASTAL CITIES

Coastal cities grew and flourished, gaining their power and glory from the Indian Ocean trade. Pangani is an ancient town that lies 28 miles (45 km) south of Tanga. Its history goes back a long way, since the time it was developed by the Arabs as a settlement and slave-trading center. Pangani had been exporting ivory, tortoise shell, coconut oil, and rhino horns since the second century B.C. Under Shirazi control, Pangani improved its fortune by selling slaves and planting groves of coconut palms. Pangani's story was typical of many similar medieval towns that were perched on the Indian Ocean, looking inland for trade goods and yet dependent on the distant country from which they had been colonized.

THE PORTUGUESE

The Portuguese, under the leadership of explorer Vasco da Gama, arrived in what is now Tanzania in 1498. The Portuguese sailors, who were on their way to and from India, were doubtless impressed by the size and civilized standards of the cities on the eastern coast, but they also considered these cities a source of competition that needed to be destroyed. They ruthlessly subdued Kilwa and Mombasa (in Kenya), virtually destroying the gold trade and showing no apparent interest in the interior of Africa.

   The Portuguese overlords preferred exacting tribute instead of settling the area permanently. After some troubled times with Turkish pirates and an increasing number of British ships, the Portuguese left. Hastening their departure were factors such as traders and raiders from Oman (on the eastern tip of Arabia), who moved into the weakened towns and established Omani Arab governors. Kilwa submitted to Omani rule in 1787.

An artist's sketch of the Portuguese arriving in Tanzania on a ship.

IN THE INTERIOR

Unobserved by the marauding foreigners on the coast, changes in the power structure far inland took place around the 18th century. Groups such as the Nyamwezi and Hehe began to move northeast and form new chiefdoms, such as the Chaga on Mount Kilimanjaro and the powerful kingdom of Usambara near the Usambara Mountains. This coastward movement was made more attractive by the development of trade. As news of this trade spread in the interior, fresh trade routes opened up toward Lake Tanganyika and the Haya kingdoms west of Lake Victoria.

Sculptures of slaves at the site of the old slave market in Zanzibar. Although the slave market in Zanzibar was closed in 1873, it took another 50 years or so to wipe out slavery from the mainland.

The separate threads of development of the coast and the interior began to be woven together.

The effect of the slave trade on East Africa must not be underestimated. While Arabs and Swahilis made fortunes from slave trading, the Nyamwezi and the Yua established their own power bases by providing porters and organizing expeditions for slaves and ivory. The large-scale capture of hundreds of thousands of Africans left some areas of East Africa virtually uninhabited. Various groups then fought over the land.

SULTAN SAYYID SAID AND ZANZIBAR

The increasing value of the trade in gold, ivory, and slaves caused Sayyid Said, the sultan of Muscat (Oman), on the Arabian peninsula, to look more carefully at the islands on the East African coast. He captured Pemba and Zanzibar. In 1832 he moved his capital to Zanzibar, probably because it was a far more pleasant place to live than dusty Oman, but also so that he could gain control over coastal towns such as Bagamoyo, through which the slave traders passed. By 1840 some 40,000 slaves were passing through the slave markets of Zanzibar each year.

The increasing call for slaves and ivory caused Arab and Swahili traders to search far inland, opening up the interior to outsiders. (Gold had been discovered in North America and Australia, and the trickle of gold from central Africa became insignificant.) There were other profitable goods as well. Sultan Said encouraged the planting of cloves on Zanzibar and Pemba, and his Zanzibari traders also made fortunes from gum copal (a resin used in making varnishes and lacquers). White traders from Europe and the Americas came to buy these goods in Zanzibar.

THE SCRAMBLE FOR AFRICA

Toward the end of the 19th century, European nations stopped sailing around the coast of Africa and turned their eyes on the huge and still uncolonized interior of Africa. They sent expeditions to claim (and, if necessary, conquer) territories to add to their growing empires in a disorganized, first-come-first-grab procedure that is often called the "Scramble for Africa."

Sultan Ibn Said Barghash was the son of Sultan Sayyid Said. His powers were greatly diminished when Germany and Britain claimed his lands.

THE SLAVE TRADE

Portugal was the first European country to meet its needs for cheap labor by using slaves. By 1460 it was importing some 700 slaves a year from trading posts on the African coast. Arab traders made fortunes shipping slaves from Africa to Arabia, Iran, and India. However, when Britain abolished the slave trade in 1807 and the United States followed suit the following year, the supply of slaves going from West Africa to British colonies and the United States almost ceased. This made the East African slave markets even more prosperous. The name of the coastal town *Bagamoyo* means "lay down your heart" because it was there that slaves would abandon their hope for freedom.

When two elephants fight, it is the grass that suffers.

—Swahili saying

The British consul in Zanzibar, John Kirk, helped end the slave trade in Zanzibar and also increased British influence in the area through the Arabs. In 1884 Dr. Carl Peters of Germany made a series of treaties with a number of inland chiefs, and the following year, Germany laid claim to the provinces of Rwanda-Burundi and what became Tanganyika. Britain retained "protectorship" over Zanzibar while Germany became the ruler of German East Africa.

GERMAN EAST AFRICA

Tanganyika as a defined area did not exist before the Germans drew its borders. It was marked on printed maps as German East Africa, and it remained so from 1890 to 1918. Carl Peters was made the imperial high commissioner of the Kilimanjaro District by German authorities. These were not happy times. There was a series of natural disasters that accompanied the harsh rule of the Germans. Resistance to German rule led to several local uprisings. The Maji-Maji Rebellion in 1905, which occurred near Kilwa in the southeast, was brutally crushed. In its wake

KING MKWAWA AND THE GERMANS

One uprising against the Germans was led by King Mkwawa, leader of the Hehe. The Hehe are the Bantu-speaking agricultural people who live in the Iringa region of southern Tanzania. King Mkwawa refused to accept the German administration and prevented German caravans from passing through what he considered Hehe land (near Iringa, set on the slopes of a cliff above the Little Ruaha River in Tanzania). In 1891 he ambushed a German patrol, killing hundreds of troops and capturing their weapons. The German response was strong and brutal. They lined up a battery of cannons against Mkwawa, who fled. After four years of guerrilla warfare, he shot himself rather than face capture.

several hundred Germans and 75,000 natives died. Areas that were once heavily populated started to return to bush and woodland.

When news of the cruel treatment of native Africans reached Germany by 1895, Carl Peters was recalled to Berlin and subsequently removed from office. His successor not only introduced laws to ensure better treatment of the local people, but also encouraged their farming efforts so that they could make a profit by growing cash crops. Their economy and living conditions were improving when World War I started in 1914. Africans were forced into a war that was not their concern. Many never returned from the war: Some died of fever, others of hunger, and others were shot during the fighting. Most of the improved conditions that had been achieved in the past had now been destroyed. The British eventually gained the upper hand against the Germans.

The Askari monument in Dar es Salaam pays tribute to the many African troops who died during World War I. It has now come to symbolize the sacrifice made by all Africans in wars not of their own making.

BRITISH TANGANYIKA

Under a League of Nations (the forerunner to the United Nations) mandate, the territories of defeated Germany were given to the countries that won World War I. Britain took responsibility for the country that was renamed Tanganyika. The British governed the country from 1919 to 1961. In their method of rule much of the local tribal and village customs were retained. After 1947 Tanganyika came under United Nations trusteeship and Britain was required to begin slowly building up the political life of Tanganyika and preparing it for eventual self-governance.

An old German headquarters in Tanzania.

The British initiated the Groundnut Scheme for peanuts in 1947. Their aim was to plant this valuable crop in vast areas of southeast Tanganyika. However, local conditions were unsuitable and all the work came to nothing.

WORLD WAR II

Although part of the World War I struggle was fought on Tanganyika's soil, causing destruction and misery, World War II had very different effects. As the world outside fought, Tanganyika got on with the business of growing food. Anything available for export was sold at a high profit. The country's export income in 1949 was six times higher than it had been when World War II began in 1939. Even more important was the way that the people thought about themselves. About 100,000 people

REVOLUTION ON ZANZIBAR

Zanzibar had become a British protectorate in 1890 and the islanders enjoyed many years of peace and prosperity. Even two world wars did not disturb the island. The island achieved independence in December 1963. Peace was overturned a month later, however, when a revolution rejected the last of the Zanzibari sultans and the black African population waged a bloody revolution to seek retribution against the Arabs for years of ill treatment.

joined the Allied forces and went to fight on the side of democracy and freedom. When they returned home they were determined that their own country would shake off its overlords and become a true, independent democracy.

The Uhuru monument is dedicated to the freedom that finally came with independence in 1961.

TOWARD INDEPENDENCE

As part of gradual preparation for Tanzania's independence, Britain appointed the first two African members to the Legislative Council in 1945. The movement toward independence gained strength after Julius Nyerere became the leader of the Tanganyika African Association (TAA) in 1953. By 1954 he had formed the Tanganyika African National Union (TANU), with the rallying slogan of *Uhuru na Umoja* ("Freedom and Unity"). After the first general election in 1958, three of the 12 cabinet ministers appointed were African, and the growing support for TANU was clear. Even successful Asian and European candidates were those supported by TANU. TANU triumphed in the 1960 election, and independence was only a year away.

NYERERE'S TANZANIA

Tanganyika became independent on December 9, 1961. The newly independent country was given new direction and dominated by Julius Nyerere, who became one of the great statesmen of Africa. His TANU party won its popularity in the first round of elections and then formed Tanganyika's first government in December 1961. Nyerere's task was to rescue a country that was suffering from poverty and lack of economic structure. In April 1964 Zanzibar and Tanganyika merged to form the United Republic of Tanzania.

There were few challenges to Nyerere's authority, particularly after he made TANU the country's only legal political party. He was highly respected in world diplomatic circles, and his opinions were respected because he preached a doctrine of blunt, hard work as the answer to economic ills. He stepped down as president in 1985, but continued as chairman of the ruling political party until 1990.

During the Nyerere years (1964–85), Tanzania stayed away from horrors such as military coups or civil wars, although Nyerere's socialism did not bring about the economic success he had hoped for. Tanzania remained one of the world's poorest countries. The salaries of upper-level government officials, including the president, were cut harshly in 1966. Julius Nyerere frequently reminded his people that they needed to work hard and be self-reliant.

WAR WITH UGANDA

The East African Community, including Tanzania, Kenya, and Uganda, was formed in 1967. It aimed to promote trade and to create travel and rail links among the three countries. By 1977, however, it had collapsed. Socialist ideas from Tanzania and capitalist ones from Kenya did not mix well; Nyerere closed Tanzania's border with Kenya in 1976. In addition, Nyerere refused to share the same table as Idi Amin, the leader of Uganda. In 1979 Tanzania went to war with Uganda after Amin sent troops to the Lake Victoria region in northern Tanzania. Tanzanian soldiers forced the troops out and then continued to march into Uganda. Amin was deposed and peace was somewhat restored, but the financial cost to Tanzania was high.

Opposite: **Julius Nyerere, president until 1985. He is often known as** *Mwalimu***, the Kiswahili word for "teacher," and occasionally as** *yule baba yetu***, meaning "that father of ours."**

THE ARUSHA DECLARATION

In 1967, in what is known as the Arusha Declaration, Nyerere set out his ideals for African socialism and his plans for rural development. Because communities were so scattered, Nyerere developed the policy of *ujamaa* (oo-JAH-mah), meaning "familyhood." His goal was to create larger, interactive communities and collective farms. At first it seemed to work. In 1975 those who had not yet formed villages were forced to do so. However, a lack of enthusiasm from the people and poor management resulted in the failure of these collective farms.

GOVERNMENT

WHEN THE TANGANYIKA AFRICAN NATIONAL UNION (TANU) was founded in 1954, Julius Nyerere and the other planners aimed to make Tanganyika self-governing. They succeeded, and on December 9, 1961, their country gained independence and became a member of the British Commonwealth. At first Nyerere guided Tanganyika as prime minister in 1961, then as president of Tanzania, formed by the union of Tanganyika and Zanzibar, in 1964. With a reputation for moderation, TANU gained the confidence of non-Africans, and Tanganyika (later as Tanzania) gradually took a leading role in African politics.

Having rid themselves of colonial rule (being ruled by a foreign power), the people wanted to rule themselves independently for the good of their own country. Julius Nyerere led them down the path of socialism (working for the benefit and betterment of their community and country) rather than communism (everything being state-owned and state-controlled). Tanzanians were taught to be suspicious of the "greed of capitalism." Nyerere's "African socialism" may have helped unite a varied population, but it was a disaster financially.

Union with Zanzibar formed the United Republic of Tanzania, which was born on April 26, 1964. From then on there were regular elections but with only one party—and one candidate—for president. Newspapers were tightly controlled. For a while only TANU party members were allowed to sell livestock in the market or to brew *pombe* (phom-BAY), the moneymaking local beer. Disagreement with the government was considered a crime, and for a while, Tanzania imprisoned political dissenters as often as the South African regime that Nyerere denounced

Above: **Supporters of Tanzania's ruling party, the CCM (Chama Cha Mapinduzi), at the 2005 elections campaign rally in Zanzibar.**

Opposite: **The Peace Memorial Museum in Zanzibar that was opened in 1925. Formerly known as the National Museum, this structure is locally known as the House of Peace.**

Village officials address-
ing the locals.

*Let others go to
the moon. We
must work to feed
ourselves.*

—*Julius Nyerere*

so vigorously. However, these days several political parties and people
are participating in the government more freely.

Zanzibar, although integrated into Tanzania's governmental and party
structure, has its own president, court system, and parliament. It continues
to exercise considerable local autonomy.

THE FAILURE OF JULIUS NYERERE'S IDEALS

Nyerere knew that there had been a time in traditional African society
when everybody was a peasant. That was his ideal, and he expressed it
in the Arusha Declaration of 1967. The widespread rural population was
supposed to join together in the collective effort of *ujamaa* ("familyhood")
communities so as to increase the output from large-scale agriculture and
easily provide social services such as water, electricity, and health clinics.
Many people were unwilling to move into these collective villages, so they
were forced to move into them. The locals tried this system, then found
that there was more opportunity for profit in the urban areas. Political
leaders were not supposed to have private incomes, but some of them

GOVERNMENT ON ZANZIBAR

Liberated from its British protectorate, Zanzibar joined the United Nations in December 1963. For 20 glorious weeks it was truly independent. Then an anti-Arab revolt deposed the sultan, and President Abeid Karume agreed to unite Zanzibar with Tanganyika to form Tanzania. Even though the harsh rule of Karume ended with his assassination in 1972, Zanzibar was under the control of the main political party of the new union, the Chama Cha Mapinduzi. To voice disagreement was considered treason, and the island's main torture center became well known for holding political dissidents.

Zanzibar has its own president. It also has its own assembly and ministries. On January 10, 1993, Zanzibar's government arranged for the island to join the Organization of the Islamic Conference. Because Zanzibar had not consulted the union government, this move was declared unconstitutional. The economic strength of Zanzibar, compared with the increasing poverty of mainland Tanzania, has created an unspoken desire for independence. The people of Zanzibar have their own history, and they want Zanzibar to be a country in its own right once again.

did. The high ideals expressed by Nyerere, the "equality of man regardless of creed or color," were not always observed, especially when it came to the 1974 confiscation of white-owned estates, which were turned into cooperative farms. Lawyers were warned that they might be deported if they represented the white landowners in court. In some cases the property that belonged to Asians was also taken over by the government.

In the late 1970s the lack of financial success of the *ujamaa* villages, combined with the ravages of drought, forced Nyerere to seek foreign aid. This meant bringing his socialist ideals in line with methods that were more acceptable to the large international aid agencies. After he was reelected as president in 1980 (again as the sole candidate), Nyerere announced that he would retire at the end of his five-year period in office.

The national flag of Tanzania combines the old Tanganyika and Zanzibar flag colors. Green stands for the land, gold for mineral wealth, black for the people, and blue for the sea.

Former president Ali Hassan Mwinyi, who was the vice president of Tanzania before becoming president of the country.

POLITICAL PARTIES

In 1977 TANU joined the Afro-Shirazi Party (which had been Zanzibar's only legal party) to form Chama Cha Mapinduzi (CCM, the Revolutionary Party of Tanzania). This was the only political party permitted in Tanzania until 1992, when President Ali Hassan Mwinyi and the CCM leadership agreed to amend the constitution. The new bill allowed multiple parties, with the condition that parties must not be formed on tribal or racial grounds. The first multiparty election was held in 1995. The CCM, the Party for Democracy and Progress (CHADEMA), the Civil United Front (CUF), the National Convention for Construction and Reform (NCCR-Mageuzi), and the Movement for a Democratic Alternative (MDA) of Zanzibar all fielded candidates. The CCM eventually won a majority in the national assembly.

PRESIDENTS MWINYI , MKAPA, AND KIKWETE

President Ali Hassan Mwinyi was elected to the office in 1985, after Nyerere resigned. He had previously been the president of Zanzibar and vice president of Tanzania. The economic situation in the country was worsening and he responded by giving more encouragement to private businesses and by accepting International Monetary Fund (IMF) proposals on budgeting and agricultural reform. Foreign aid began to arrive as Mwinyi reassured investors that he was serious about economic reform. He even dismissed several government ministers who had apparently opposed his economic plans. However, Mwinyi was later accused of corruption, and a code of ethics was introduced by popular demand. This code required officeholders to declare their wealth and how they acquired it. Mwinyi ran as the only presidential candidate in 1990 and was reelected.

In 1994 a corrupt scheme for avoiding as much as $70 million a year in import tax was uncovered. The IMF promptly froze all aid to Tanzania and did not resume payments until 1996. Meanwhile the first election without a one-party system had occurred (in October 1995), although there had been some accusations of vote rigging in Zanzibar and elsewhere. In June 1996 Mwinyi stepped down as national chairman of the CCM political party. Minister of Science, Technology, and Higher Education Benjamin Mkapa, a former journalist, diplomat, and foreign minister, was chosen to be Mwinyi's successor as leader of the party. With the opposition parties split in their votes, Mkapa was then elected president of Tanzania with the backing of Nyerere, who vouched for his honesty.

Mkapa sought economic growth through foreign investments. He privatized most of the state-owned corporations and pursued free-market policies. The World Bank and IMF supported his policies and canceled some of Tanzania's foreign debts. However, Mkapa was not above criticism. His lavish spending on his presidential jet and military equipment drew public outrage.

Jakaya Kikwete began his presidency in 2005.

Jakaya Kikwete took office as the fourth president of Tanzania on December 21, 2005. President Kikwete's governing philosophy and political views have been influenced by those of Mwalimu Julius Nyerere, with whom Kikwete was close. So far Kikwete's government has received accolades across the country and from the donor community for fighting corruption, investing in people—particularly in education, and for pushing for new investments.

PARLIAMENT

The constitution of Tanzania (which was revised in 1984) establishes the offices of president and vice president. The president is chief of state, head

37

of government, and commander in chief of the armed forces. Zanzibar elects a president, who becomes the head of the Revolutionary Government of Zanzibar. He governs matters internal to Zanzibar and also upholds the constitution of the United Republic of Tanzania.

The 274 members of the National Assembly are chosen on the basis of a complex formula that includes directly elected members from the mainland and Zanzibar as well as allocated seats for women, for members appointed by the National Assembly and by the president, and for appointed regional commissioners. Zanzibar has its own House of Representatives, which makes laws especially for Zanzibar.

A general election must be held at least once every five years. Under the revised constitution a president may not serve more than two terms of office (of five years each). The United Republic of Tanzania has 26 administrative regions: 21 on the mainland, three on Zanzibar, and two on Pemba.

A woman casts her vote in the 2005 elections in Stone Town in Tanzania.

JUSTICE

Tanzania has an independent judiciary with a four-level system of primary courts, district magistrate courts, the high court, and the court of appeal. The chief justice is head of the court of appeal, which is located in Dar es Salaam. Zanzibar has its own courts. The highest judicial authority there is the Supreme Council.

There is a network of courts throughout the country. The legal system includes English, Islamic, and customary law. At the most basic level, the courts often deal with matters of traditional custom. There was, for example, a husband who demanded a refund of cattle from his bride-price because his wife had given birth to only one child, but the case was settled in favor of the bride's parents. (The institution of bride-price or bride-wealth specifies that a prospective husband, usually with the help of his relatives, must provide a substantial sum of money or highly valued goods to his future wife's family before a marriage can be contracted). Recent legislation has given women more opportunity to seek justice.

The political headquarters of the CCM party in Dodoma.

FOREIGN POLICY

Tanzania is a member of the United Nations (UN) and the African Union. It is also a member of the Southern African Development Community (SADC), which is interested in creating a more integrated common market among its member countries.

Despite his stated ideals of African unity, Nyerere believed that it was the duty of African leaders to intervene when neighboring countries were heading in the wrong direction. He helped topple three neighboring governments: Comoros in 1975, Seychelles in 1977, and Uganda in 1978 to 1979. Some 60,000 Tanzanian troops formed an "army of liberation" and joined Ugandan opposition forces (supporting Milton Obote, who was the former prime minister [1962–66] and president [1966–71, 1980–85] of Uganda) to defeat the brutal dictator Idi Amin and his Libyan allies in 1979. However, the Organization of African Unity condemned Tanzania's action as "interference in the affairs of a member state." Tanzania had to bear the expenses for the military action alone—a bill of over $500 million. In November 1993 the presidents of Tanzania, Uganda, and Kenya signed a protocol to renew cooperation among their countries.

Justice in Zanzibar today is a welcome improvement over the system of justice 100 years ago, when those who committed the worst crimes were publicly beheaded with a sword.

39

DODOMA

Although most of the government administration is based in Tanzania's largest city, Dar es Salaam, Dodoma was the country's official capital until 1974. Dodoma was planned to showcase Nyerere's ideal of all ethnic groups living together in a shared sense of *ujamaa* ("togetherness" or "familyhood"). According to a 2002 census Dodoma has 376,530 households.

Dodoma was a small trading center for many years, with caravan traders passing through the city. It grew in importance when the Germans decided to build the Central Railway Line, which runs from Dar es Salaam to Kigoma, through Dodoma.

On the map Dodoma appears to be conveniently central, a stopping point on the east-west railway and a north-south trunk road. It also has an airport. However, Dodoma is an uncomfortable place to live, is fairly dry and windy, and has a limited water supply. So far only the party political headquarters of the CCM has moved there.

Since 1990 Tanzania has created an environment designed to attract foreigners to invest, trade, and tour the country by implementing socioeconomic liberalization policies and institutional reforms. One such reform is the establishment and expansion of the private sector, which Tanzania recognizes as the engine that drives economic development and sustainability. Under the country's diplomatic missions abroad, the government has opened trade centers to work closely with the Tanzania Tourist Board, Parastatal Sector Reform Commission, and the Tanzanian Investment Center.

DEFENSE

Tanzanian troops are used mainly to enforce law and order, but they also saw active service in the war against Uganda. Many troops are on patrol in the troubled border region around the Great Lakes. Young men who complete secondary school at 18 years of age must serve in the military for two years. This service may include working on civil projects.

The Tanzanian air force was initially built up with help from Canada, with combat equipment that had been purchased from China. Tanzania has been a participant in several peacekeeping efforts on the African continent: in the military coup that led to a full-scale civil war in Liberia in 1995, in Lebanon in 2006, and to end the genocide that has pitted African and Arab tribes of Darfur in Sudan against each other. Tanzania's military expenditures amounted to $6 million in 2003.

Tanzania considered itself one of the frontline states—being a country situated on the border of a war-threatened area—in opposition to South Africa and its policy of apartheid. It was the first country to welcome the African National Congress (Nelson Mandela's political party) when it was banned in South Africa.

AND TODAY?

Although it does not have a strong economy or military, Tanzania is at peace and is becoming more respected in African politics. The Tanzania Development Vision 2025—a team of experts appointed to come up with strategies to develop the country—was developed to rekindle the hopes and expectations of Tanzanians as well as their patriotism and nationalistic aspirations. It envisions that, by the year 2025, Tanzanian society will be free from poverty and will have graduated from being one of the world's least-developed countries to being one of the middle-income countries, with a high level of amenities development. The six main attributes of the development vision include high-quality livelihood, peace, stability and unity, good governance, a well-educated and more aware society, and a competitive economy that is capable of producing sustainable growth and shared benefits.

Army soldiers practicing their drills in Zanzibar.

ECONOMY

SINCE THE DAYS of German and British colonialism, Tanzania has not been a rich country. It plunged into economic disaster in the 1970s, then climbed out of trouble with huge injections of foreign aid. Today it still ranks among the poorest countries of the world—although, in African terms, it is a paradise when compared to Madagascar or the Democratic Republic of Congo (formerly called Zaire). Tanzania's per capita income in 2006 was estimated to be about $320. Most Tanzanians exist on what they can produce for themselves—this is called subsistence living. Their agricultural resources (such as coffee, cloves, and cashew nuts) could prosper if world demand grew high enough. Tanzania also has mineral resources (including diamonds, gold, and gypsum), although these are found in limited quantities. There are also increasing opportunities for tourism. Still Tanzania is basically a poor country.

THE ROUTE TO DISASTER

President Nyerere, through his ideas regarding communal *ujamaa* villages, concentrated on the uplift of ordinary people who were struggling to survive in the widespread rural areas of Tanzania. Banks, hotels, and large businesses were supposed to be nationalized (owned by the government) and run by the state for the good of the whole country. Unfortunately his plan did not work, largely because of poor management and corruption. Many people lost their incentive to succeed under Nyerere's plan. Anyone who earned a high salary was taxed at the incredibly high rate of 95 percent of their income, which made people reluctant to work hard. In addition, world oil prices escalated, the East African Economic Community

Above: **Local fishermen sorting through their catch at Dar es Salaam.**

Opposite: **Refined copper bars being loaded on cranes to be exported.**

*The World Bank
has helped
Tanzania improve
the quality and
efficiency of the
power systems in
Dar es Salaam,
Arusha, and
Kilimanjaro
with a $111
million project
that gave 81,000
rural and urban
homes and public
services access to
electricity.*

collapsed, and Tanzania spent a fortune on the invasion of Uganda. By the late 1980s Tanzania was one of the largest recipients of financial aid in the world.

AGRICULTURE

There was a time when the soil of Tanzania was fertile enough to produce regular small crops to feed its scattered small communities. Then came *ujamaa*, the gathering of the people together in larger communities that required more concentrated farming of the land, followed by plantations and cash-crop farming. Today some 80 percent of the workforce is engaged in agriculture, which contributes 40 percent of the gross domestic product (GDP) of Tanzania.

Women winnowing rice, one of the main food crops. The rice is tossed into the air so the wind will separate the husk from the grain.

44

Much of Tanzania's more systematic and successful agriculture was started by the German settlers who researched cultivation methods. They found a means of controlling the tsetse fly that was preventing human settlement in many infested areas. They also introduced sisal, cotton, coffee, and tea as crops.

Only 4 percent of Tanzania's land is suitable for farming because of its topography, poor soil, and little rainfall. The majority of the agriculture is subsistence farming (where farmers just grow food for themselves to eat) and is the only source of food for the 12 million people who live on corn, sorghum, millet, rice, peas, beans, and other vegetables. Yet agricultural products are Tanzania's main exports, making up around 80 percent of all exported goods.

Coffee, sugar, and cashew nuts were the most important cash crops in 2006. The reduction of state interference in rural marketing has encouraged more farmers to grow cash crops for local sale. Sisal is also a major cash crop. The leaves of the sisal plant produce a hairy white fiber from which rope, string, and coarse mats are made. The port of Tanga, on the Indian Ocean, depends on the sisal trade, and the country inland is covered with huge rectangular plantations of sisal. Sisal is exported mostly in raw form, because wealthy nations in Europe and elsewhere put an extra import charge on rope, preventing Tanzania from making its own rope from sisal and selling it at a higher price. The use of synthetic fibers has reduced the demand for sisal.

In recent years the number of private investors in the agriculture sector increased by 20 percent. Farmers have been trained in the use of irrigation technology and equipment, animal husbandry, and the preparation and

A worker arranges treated sisal to dry on a rack.

CLOVES

Tanzania is one of the world's main suppliers of cloves. Dried clove buds are used to flavor food. The oil that is obtained through steam distillation is used in dentistry as an anesthetic and also in cigarettes, foodstuffs, and toiletries.

Cloves were introduced to Zanzibar from Southeast Asia—probably Indonesia—around 1832. Through the labor of slaves, Zanzibar quickly developed a flourishing trade in cloves. Although Zanzibar has been called "the island of cloves," a larger harvest now comes from the island of Pemba, north of Zanzibar. When two-thirds of the clove trees on Zanzibar were destroyed in a hurricane in 1872, Pemba took over as the main producer of cloves. Today Pemba accounts for 90 percent of cloves grown from a combined total of 3.5 million clove trees. Many of the trees are owned by small-scale farmers and have been owned by the farmers' families for generations. The clove industry has declined due to falling prices caused by the advent of food-refrigeration technology and a decrease in demand for preservatives and spices.

Every part of the clove tree—its leaves, flowers, and bark—has an aroma, but it is the sun-dried flower buds that are actually known as cloves and used to flavor foods such as apple pie. The oil of cloves is also used in perfumes and soaps. The unopened buds of the clove tree are picked and spread out on the ground to dry for about five days. While the cloves are being harvested, all schools are closed, and everyone helps with the harvesting.

use of fertilizers in the production of vegetables. Research centers focus on crops and the production of seed varieties that are drought- and pest- resistant.

TRADE

Because the majority of locally produced food and manufactured goods are for home consumption, Tanzania's export trade is never much, and vital imports often cost more than the country can afford. If the economy improves, Tanzania may attract foreign investors. The principal exports from the mainland are gold, coffee, cashew nuts, manufactures, and cotton. From Zanzibar and Pemba come a large part of the world's supply of cloves and clove oil.

The main imports are consumer goods, machinery, transportation equipment, industrial raw materials, and crude oil. Dar es Salaam is by far the main port, with several deepwater berths, a bulk oil jetty, and a wharf for one- or two-masted sailing dhows and schooners. Trade is also carried out at Zanzibar, Tanga, and Mtwara, and at ports around Lake Victoria, Tanganyika, and Nyasa. Tanzania is free of ideological confrontations, ethnic problems, and labor disputes. Access to low cost labor and the government's commitment to developing skilled labor and trained specialists are some of the success factors listed in Tanzania's improvement index report.

MINING AND INDUSTRY

Women sorting out cashew nuts at a cashew processing factory in Dar es Salaam.

Tanzania's mining has been dominated by the diamond mine at Mwadui, found by Dr. J. T. Williamson in 1940. After his death in 1958 all shares of this mine were bought and divided equally between the Tanzanian government and De Beers Consolidated Mines. In that year diamonds ranked as the country's fourth-leading export.

Some gold has been mined near Lake Victoria, and prospectors have discovered fresh gold reefs in the Kahama District, south of Lake Victoria. The Buhemba, the Bulyanhulu, the Geita, the Golden Pride, and the North Mara mines had a combined capacity to produce about 125,223 pounds (56,800 kg) of gold per year. Semiprecious stones such as corundum, zircon, and amethyst, as well as tin and mica, are also available in small quantities. Valuable deposits of coal and iron exist in the south, but their development as an asset is hampered by the poor access roads.

Manufacturing export is a third important sector in foreign exchange earnings, after agriculture and tourism. Until 1999 about 48 percent of total monthly wage earners—or 140,000 people—were employed in industries such as food and beverage processing, textiles, wooden products, paper products, chemicals, plastics, jewelry, and hand tools. Most electricity is produced by hydroelectric plants: Much power comes from the Mtera and Kidatu dams on the Great Ruaha River. A drought in 2004 reduced hydroelectric output to half its full capacity. This led to the implementation of the World Bank–funded Emergency Power Plan.

In the past machines and equipment were frequently abandoned because few people had the technical knowledge to repair them. Today education in science and technology and a good number of research and development institutions are in place in most sectors. These institutions include the University of Dar es Salaam, Sokoine University of Agriculture, and the University College of Lands and Architectural Studies, which became a constituent college of the University of Dar es Salaam (UDSM) on July 1, 1996. Examples of research and development (R&D) and science and technology (S&T) service institutions are the Center for Agricultural Mechanization and Rural Technology, the National Institute of Medical Research, and the Serengeti Wildlife Research Institute.

Following the escalation of oil prices in 2006, the prices of petroleum products in the domestic market also increased.

A miner resting outside a mining field, near the base of Mount Kilimanjaro in Tanzania.

TOURISM

The government created the Tanzania Tourist Board to try to market the country's wildlife attractions while also focusing on environmental protection. Development in national parks is done in consultation with the World Conservation Union. The rewards for the economy are good: An attempt to climb Kilimanjaro will cost a visitor at least $600, with no guarantee that he or she will get to the top! Big tourist companies whisk visitors around the northern safari circuit of Serengeti National Park, Ngorongoro Conservation Area, Lake Manyara, Tarangire, Arusha National Park, and Kilimanjaro National Park, all within a few days, although too many vehicles in one spot can raise dust clouds, which affects good game viewing. Venturing south, one quickly discovers the splendors of the Ruaha and Selous game reserves, Mikumi and Udzungwa mountain national parks, and the almost untouched southern beaches. Marine tourism—for diving and fishing—is also gaining popularity.

Tourists getting up close with the African wildlife during a safari ride at the Ngorongoro Conservation area.

Tanzania can boost its tourism industry by increasing the number of flights into the country, and by providing quality service and sufficient accommodations around the national parks for its visitors. According to Tanzania's tourism board, 644,124 visitors came to Tanzania in 2006, boosting the country's earnings by 4 percent (or $862 million), compared to the previous year. Participation in international tourism fairs is done annually in order to open new markets. An important attraction is cultural tourism, which is related to archives and antiquities. Visits by locals and foreigners to national museums have increased steadily.

Buses, trucks, and trailers stopping by a gas station in Tanzania.

TRANSPORTATION

Buses are the main means of transportation in Tanzania, although many roads are not in good condition and are not necessarily tarred. They vary from usable to impassable. The Tanzam Highway was built as a joint venture between the Tanzanian and Zambian governments. Once known as the hell run, it was recently resurfaced. This road links the southwest of the country with Dar es Salaam. Roads in poorer districts are riddled with potholes, and the traffic wanders around on whatever flat surface is left. *Matatus* (ma-TAH-toos), the most heavily used buses, are usually crammed with people and their goods. *Dala dala* (DAA-la DAA-la), which include minivans, pickup trucks, and old four-wheel-drive vehicles, are the standard way to get around towns.

There are two railway systems: the Tazara line from Dar es Salaam, which runs south via Mbeya to New Kapiri Mposhi in Zambia, and the Central Line, which heads west to Kigoma and Mwanza via Tabora, and Lakes Tanganyika and Victoria. The western line is the artery of Tanzania's heartland. Built by the Germans before World War I, it runs as straight as a highway across many miles of savannah plateau.

Dar es Salaam is the major port, with three-fourths of all ships that sail to Tanzania calling there. In the Indian Ocean dhows and motorboats ply between coastal towns and islands, including a hydrofoil ferry service to Zanzibar. Tanzanians who live near one of the Great Lakes travel by ferry to destinations along the shores. The historic MV (Motor Vessel) *Liemba*, which may be the oldest steamer in regular service, has huffed and puffed up and down Lake Tanganyika since 1914.

Air Tanzania connects Dar es Salaam with Zanzibar, Kilimanjaro, Bukoba, and Mwanza. A number of private airlines operate six- to eight-seaters. A number of international airlines fly to Dar es Salaam, and a few touch down at Kilimanjaro and Zanzibar.

TODAY AND THE FUTURE

Much of Tanzania's tax money was used to pay interest on foreign aid or to pay state workers. It was difficult to develop much of an infrastructure as a result. In early 1997 a crippling drought followed one in 1992 that affected parts of Somalia, eastern Kenya, and northern Tanzania. The country's budget had to be revised to provide emergency spending for drought victims, as some 4 million people faced food emergencies.

Today the country's tax money is used to strengthen the infrastructure by financing the construction of schools and hospitals and the provision of essential utilities such as electricity and running water. It seems that Tanzania has managed to maintain an image of what liberal-minded donors think an African country should be: socialist, full of ideals, and sufficiently free from corruption. Tanzania's 2006 to 2007 budget consisted of 39 percent funding from foreign sources. The World Bank recently approved more than $230 million in credit to Tanzania to support the government's strategy for economic growth and poverty reduction. The funds will be used to increase school enrollment and literacy rates, reduce child and maternal mortality, increase access to safe water, and strengthen sustainable development efforts.

ENVIRONMENT

THE SURVIVAL OF MANKIND depends largely on humans' ability to sustain a harmonious relationship with the natural elements. Poverty, urbanization, and rapid demographic growth have upset the delicate balance between environmental resources and pollution in the last century. In an effort to reverse the trend of environmental degradation, the government of Tanzania established the National Environment Management Council (NEMC) in 1983 to ensure that the basic needs of the present and future generations are met without risking people's health or safety. Various programs have been implemented in both rural and urban areas to educate people and cultivate interest in environmental management and conservation. This is done through radio, television, and the press.

LAND DEGRADATION

Over 90 percent of the Tanzanian population is rural and depends on land resources for its livelihood. Farmers, who are also landholders, are

Left: **A view of the Serengeti National Park in Arusha. The park is home to many species of animals, and very popular with tourists.**

Opposite: **Every year, thousands of flamingos use Lake Magadi in the Ngorongoro Crater of Arusha as a breeding ground.**

Livestock in a rural farm. Overgrazing has become a problem in Tanzania as farmers increase the size of their herd, causing land degradation to take place.

aware that declining soil fertility is linked to poor farming practices, deforestation, and overgrazing. Places at risk of soil erosion and decline include Dodoma, Shinyanga, Mwanza, Arusha, and Tabora. Another factor that leads to land degradation is overgrazing. Where the size of livestock is an indicator of wealth, farmers tend to maximize their herd size. Conservation experts are developing a package to improve crop and livestock practices, tailored and fine-tuned to the needs of the farmers.

WATER POLLUTION

Tanzania faces water shortages and poor water quality, even though the country is blessed with a wide variety of water resources. One reason for this is that water is contaminated by disposal and leakage from industrial activity. Dar es Salaam, which hosts most of the country's industrial activity, faces major pollution from sewage, solid waste, and industrial waste. It is estimated that almost 75 percent of the industries of Tanzania are located in the coastal areas, and they pollute the Indian Ocean. Laws have been put in place to prevent further pollution.

The Msimbazi River flows across one-third of Dar es Salaam. It is important to some 100,000 people who live in the area. Water here is used for drinking, bathing, agriculture, and industry. To minimize industrial and domestic pollution, the government, in partnership with environmental and conservation agencies, has conducted water analysis to determine the sources of pollution. In 2003 the government began a $164.6 million project to renovate and expand the Dar es Salaam sewage system.

Mwanza, a city located on Lake Victoria, has been experiencing increasing pollution from factories and mines that are discharging untreated waste into the lake. Waste from fish-processing plants, oil-processing plants, textile plants, and tanneries is released untreated directly into Lake Victoria. So is domestic waste. Radio and television programs are being used to address industrial pollution issues and help in the enforcement of environmental laws.

LOSS OF WILDLIFE HABITAT AND BIODIVERSITY

The spread of intensive agriculture, leading to fragmentation and elimination of the forests, may have caused some plants and animals to become extinct. Loss of wildlife habitat and biodiversity in Tanzania

Women balancing buckets used to fetch the household water. As this family requires 20 buckets a day, these women have to walk a great distance before lining up to get them.

arises mainly from the increasing demand for fuel wood, charcoal, and wood to be used as raw material for rural and urban industries.

The use of pesticides also contributes to the loss of biodiversity. One example is the slopes of Kilimanjaro, which produces the famous arabica coffee. It has been the backbone of the native economy for more than 100 years. In the early 1970s a disease commonly called the Coffee Berry Disease attacked the coffee crop. The disease hits the coffee berries before they mature. Huge amounts of pesticides were used to combat the disease. In a very short time, butterflies, bees, birds, and reptiles disappeared from the area. Tanzania tends to focus its conservation efforts on bigger animals such as elephants; not enough is done for bird species (which number around 1,500) and plant species (which number more than 10,000) that are disappearing rapidly.

As conservation efforts center around the larger animals in the savannah, such as the black rhinoceros in the Ngorongoro Conservation Area, very little is done for the smaller animals.

In the Zanzibar archipelago, the biggest threat to the region's marine ecosystem is illegal fishing, which is done with destructive gear such as dragnets and small mesh nets. Fishermen use poles to break corals and hunt endangered sea turtles. There is also the threat of overfishing certain species, such as chango and kingfish. Traditional conservation messages were ignored until these fishermen learned the ways of conservation from the Koran—the sacred text of Islam, believed by Muslims to record the revelations of God to the Prophet Muhammad.

Local and nongovernmental organizations pioneered the project, using Muslim environmental ethics. Fishermen who want to give up their trade are being helped to find alternative ways to earn a living. The program has helped fishermen and their families through a credit and savings program to grow and sell produce, tend beehives, and make handicrafts.

A poster encouraging the locals to take care of their environment.

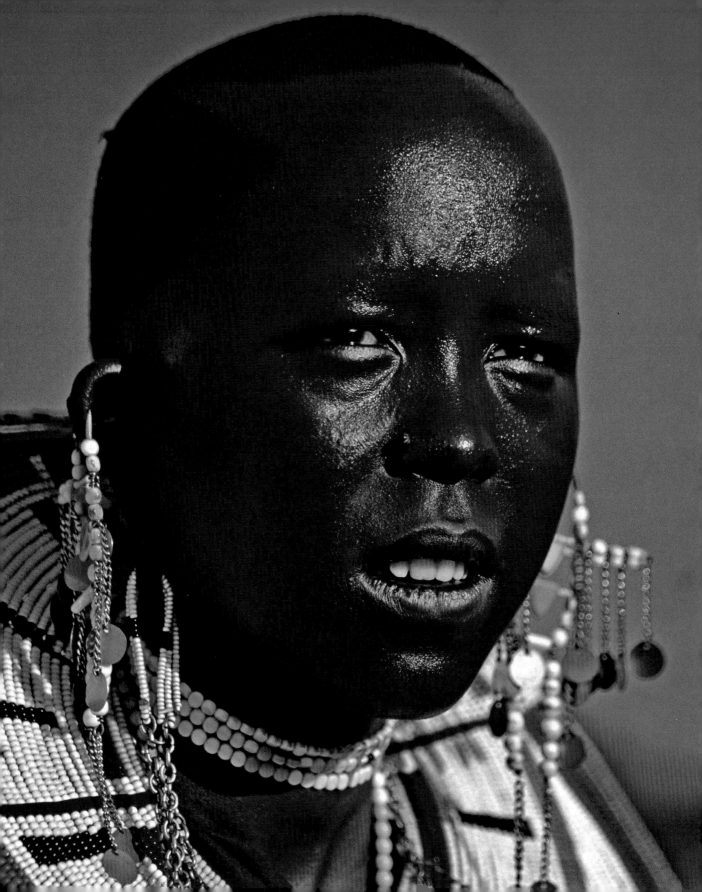

TANZANIANS

GEOGRAPHY WAS one of the earliest influences on Tanzania's population. Those living on the inland plateau came from within Africa, while settlers along the Indian Ocean coast came from outside. Low rainfall and the tsetse fly have created several sparsely populated areas in the interior. As a result two-thirds of the population live only in the northern part of the country. In the past slave caravans probed relentlessly into the interior and built up wealth and populations on the coast. Yet Tanzania is still one of the least urbanized countries of Africa, with only 23 percent of its people living in towns. In Zanzibar the urban population is 40 percent, according to the 2002 census.

Unlike many other African countries Tanzania is not dominated by any one ethnic group. So there is no warfare or striving for dominance among the tribes, although there are struggles for power between Christians and Muslims. Tribes such as the Chaga and Haya, which came under Christian missionary influence in the colonial days, have a higher representation in the power structure than would seem appropriate to their numbers.

There are an estimated 120 different black African tribal groups in Tanzania. There are also small communities of Indian, Pakistani, European, and Arab people.

Left: **A tribesman with his herd of goats.**

Opposite: **A Masai woman with her shaven head, painted face, and elaborate coils of beads over her neck and shoulders.**

A man from the Makonde tribe carving in the markets of Tanzania.

Presently the days of Masai spears and Hehe muzzle-loaders are over. These days men carry a carved walking stick; a long, straight stick (useful for prodding cattle); or a rolled, black umbrella.

THE MAIN ETHNIC GROUPS

SUKUMA South and west of Lake Victoria live the Sukuma people, who represent between 15 and 20 percent of Tanzania's population. Once fierce warriors who would prove their manhood by spearing a lion, they now live more peaceably, tending cattle and growing staple crops such as millet, sorghum, and corn in the fertile land around Mwanza. Cotton was added as a cash crop in recent years.

MASAI These famous nomadic warriors of the past now live in the Serengeti, Ngorongoro Crater, and Masai Mara areas, in small settlements of eight to 15 huts per *kraal*—an enclosure for livestock—tending their precious herds of cattle, sheep, and goat. Although the Masai are often thought of as a Kenyan people, there are probably more Masai living in Tanzania than in Kenya.

CHAGA On the southern slopes of Kilimanjaro, north of Masai country, live the enterprising Chaga people. Their distinctive beehive-shaped thatched huts are disappearing fast, because the Chaga are a businesslike group who are making an increasing financial profit by supplying guides and porters for the tourists who wish to explore what the Chaga consider their mountain. They also tend prosperous farms and coffee plantations on Kilimanjaro's fertile slopes.

SWAHILI Called *Waswahili* in the language itself, *Swahili* means "the coastal people." Because of their mixed African and Arab ancestry, the Swahili look more brownish-gold than black, and their bone structure often shows a more European profile. Their language, Kiswahili, is the national language, or official language, in Tanzania, Kenya, and Congo (DRC).

GOGO Based around Dodoma, the Gogo tend herds and plant crops in a land that is desperate for water. Many still wear little more than a flowing *kanga* cloth, and their earlobes are bright with rings of copper wire. One hundred years ago they were strong enough to halt the advance of the Masai, but now their numbers are shrinking.

NYAMWEZI The Nyamwezi people's name means "people of the moon," and they were one of the most powerful tribes met by Western explorers such as David Livingstone and Henry Morton Stanley. They live in the western savannah in and around Tabora, to the south of Lake Victoria.

A man from the Ha tribe squats by the doorway of his grass hut.

HAYA Northwest of the Nyamwezi are the tea and coffee plantations of the Haya. The Haya reside around the western shore of Lake Victoria. Haya women produce excellent craftwork. The Haya were successful traders even before the arrival of the Europeans.

MAKONDE Famous for their woodcarving, the Makonde people live on a high inland plateau on the border with Mozambique, in southern Tanzania near the eastern shores of Lake Nyasa. Regarded with a

These rural women with their head loads have features of the Bantu type.

The word Hehe *is said to have originated from the battle cry— "hee-hee"—of the most famous Hehe chief, Mkwawa, who led years of resistance against German colonizers in the Iringa area of central Tanzania.*

superstitious respect by the surrounding tribes, some of the Makonde men file their teeth to sharp points and create elaborate scar patterns on their bodies

HEHE Once feared and warlike, many of the Hehe now work as rangers and guides. They were one of very few tribes to claim major victories against the German colonial armies.

HA The largest town on the shores of Lake Tanganyika, Kigoma, is home to the Ha tribe. Living in a withdrawn forest world of mystic beliefs, the Ha are known for their marathon dance celebrations, which may go on through several days and nights. They are cattle herders who still dress in natural materials.

NATIONAL CHARACTERISTICS

Some 60 million black Africans are sometimes referred to as *Bantu*, a name that also describes the related group of languages that they speak.

REFUGEES

There are now fewer than half a million refugees in Tanzania from the Burundi and Democratic Republic of Congo. In 1993 a failed coup attempt in Burundi (after the democratically elected Hutu government had taken office) sent a wave of refugees into Tanzania's Kigoma and Kagera regions in the northwest. More refugees came after the outbreak of civil war in Rwanda in April 1994. The Tanzanian government had granted a few refugees the right to reside outside the camps for educational, medical, or security reasons, but most refugees are restricted to gathering firewood within about 2.5 miles (4 km) of the camps. As the supplies closer to home become depleted, the refugees venture farther, unprotected against bandits, physical abuse, and rape.

The Tanzanian government encourages these refugees to return to their home countries because the situations of war, murder, and tribal conflict that they originally ran away from no longer exist.

The word *bantu* means simply "the men." It comes from the word *ntu*, meaning "man," and the plural prefix *ba-*. Although they mixed through the centuries with other ethnic groups (such as Arabs, Persians, and Indians), most Tanzanians are of the Bantu type, with dark brown skin (varying between black and tan-colored), a broad face with high cheekbones, and a powerful, muscular physique. The Masai, however, are from the Nilotic group of tribes that originally migrated in from north of Tanzania. While the government has discouraged many tribal practices in order to create a sense of national identity, the Masai people still retain many of their traditional customs.

SEPARATE COMMUNITIES

In Dar es Salaam and along the coast, where Africa comes up against the ideas of the outside world more forcibly, there is frequent conflict between African Tanzanians and Asian Tanzanians. The Asians make

The Tanzanians cling to their respect for authority. The president's picture is displayed in offices, restaurants, and schools everywhere— usually alongside pictures of Julius Nyerere.

up most of the merchant/business class and, as a result, are often wealthier. The few wealthy Africans are primarily government officials.

The various communities live in different ways and have their own customs. They may all drink together in bars and play games together, but the racial communities tend to live apart and marry within their own community.

CLOTHING

Glossy brochures like to show Africans in traditional robes, beaded necklaces, and oversized earrings. The truth, however, is that most Tanzanian men wear T-shirts and jeans, much like people all over the world, often choosing bright colors. Richer businessmen may favor an open-necked white shirt with a dark suit. Modern European-style clothing is seen by many Tanzanians as a sign of progress, and sometimes as an indication that a family has become Christian. Even those Tanzanians who wear a traditional wrap draped over the shoulder will often wear a modern dress or trousers underneath. Known as a *kanga* (KAN-gah) on the coast, this wrap consists of a long, straight length of brightly patterned cotton. This is cut in two

A woman selling modern clothes favored by the younger generation in Tanzania.

so that one-half is wound around the body below the armpit and the other is draped over the shoulders or head by women over their other clothing. Poorer folk who live inland will keep a clean dress or *kanga* to wear to church or to a party in the local beer club, while for the normal working day, an old wrapper will do.

There are, of course, regional differences in clothing. In the predominantly Muslim areas along the eastern coast and on Zanzibar,

THE MASAI

The Masai scorn modern styles and stand proudly in red blankets, with their bodies and plaited hair smeared with red ochre and sheep fat. Men and women have elongated earlobes, hung with metal ornaments, and they wear rows of beaded necklaces. Although the tall lion-spear is now forbidden, every Masai man carries a weapon of some sort. The young men go through a coming of age ceremony to become *moran*, or warriors.

The Masai may not be typical of Tanzania as a whole, but they represent the pride of Africa, with their continued refusal to be altered by Western civilization. Although many of the other tribes have been encouraged to modernize their ways in the interests of national identity, the Masai have been allowed to continue their traditional lifestyle. According to their folklore all the cattle in the world rightly belong to them, because *Ngai*, their sole god, had given the cattle to the Masai. The Masai's duty was to protect the herds of their people and, logically, to capture other people's cattle. Cattle represent the owner's wealth and are very rarely killed.

The Masai still remain an essentially nomadic people, moving with the seasons over a great stretch of open, dry country, and frequently ignoring modern impositions such as national borders or the boundaries of game reserves. They are only slowly coming to accept changes in their lifestyle.

the men wear the *kanzu*, an ankle-length white robe with a little fine embroidery at neck and hem, with a red fez or a white embroidered Muslim cap. Some Muslim women wear a large piece of black calico (*bui-bui*) thrown over their heads like a hood, a requirement for modesty in Islam, but below this may wear far more colorful clothing. In more traditional style some women hide their faces from the sight of all men (other than their husbands), except for an eye-slit located between their headscarf and robe. Others, however, leave their face uncovered.

BY WESTERN STANDARDS, Tanzania is a poor, struggling country where the majority of people live close to subsistence level. What money becomes available seems to go to the few rather than to the many. Yet, by African standards, rural Tanzanians are better off than the people in many neighboring countries. There is a network of schools, health-care centers, and marketing cooperatives, even if supplies and standards are limited.

The countryside today is a mix of *ujamaa* communities, traditional isolated villages, state farms, and private estates. Many younger people are moving into the cities, although there are few jobs. The children of some city families have to drop out of school and work so there will be enough food. When people in the city do manage to gather enough money, they normally go home to the country, where they buy land and houses. In this way they create security for their old age.

Above: **A busy city scene in Dar es Salaam.**

Opposite: **Masai children washing in a basin outside their home in Dodoma.**

VILLAGE LIFE

Village life can be hard, and it can be a struggle to make ends meet. Most families live in one-story homes with corrugated iron roofs shaded by banana palms. If the family has enough money, the outside of the house is painted. The women do most of the work, as well as bearing and bringing up the children. The necessities of life have not changed. Women still work the fields and prepare the food; men go fishing, tend cattle, work on a plantation, or build houses or fences. Most of each day is spent finding enough food to eat and water to drink. Without any apparent effort, a woman will carry a heavy plastic water container

On the rare evening when a party is held, benches are set out beneath banana trees and meat is roasted on an open fire. The adults sit around drinking banana pombe *(PHOM-bay) or European beer.*

Many of Tanzania's young people are heading toward the urban areas looking for employment.

or loaded woven basket on her head with a twisted cloth underneath for padding and balance. The children work, too. Girls guard the fields against birds and help their mothers with the planting, washing, sweeping, and fetching water. Boys as young as seven or eight years old go out with their fathers to fish or tend coconut trees, or carry tools.

If there is time for recreation, children play at being adults—the girls may play with sand, pretending they are pounding and cooking rice. They make up songs and dances while the boys drum on a log. The first meal of the day is eaten around 2:00 P.M., after the mother returns with water and wood to start a fire. The rest of the afternoon, the women are busy washing clothes, processing rice or cassava—a shrubby, tropical, perennial plant—and plaiting mats until after 8:00 P.M. when prayers are said and the evening meal is eaten.

URBAN LIFE

The urban population is growing at about 10 percent each year, yet city jobs are so scarce that the government has been known to take truckloads of people, sometimes at gunpoint, back to the rural areas. No one has been sure whether the people were being forced to live in *ujamaa* villages or were merely being removed from overcrowded cities. There is no such thing as unemployment benefits in Tanzania. People say, "*Mnyonge hana haki* (A poor person has no rights)." Most try to sell something: *mradi* (mRAH-dee) or petty trade, either in handfuls of nuts, a fish, single cigarettes, or bundles of charcoal. Small-scale beer brewing brings in quick money, although it is illegal.

THE MANY USES OF COCONUTS

The white meat inside coconuts is dried to produce copra, which is the dried kernel of the coconut, and rope and string are made from its fibrous husk. Apart from these commercial uses, the coconut provides a handy takeaway meal and its juice a refreshing drink—it can be quite alcoholic if allowed to ferment, when it is called *tembo* (TAM-boh). Copra produces an oil that is used for cooking, hair care, or to make soap and candles. The dried fronds of the coconut tree are used for thatching roofs and to weave mats, screens, and baskets. The attractively grained timber is used for making ornaments. In all, the coconut is vital to the people of the coast.

Where one all-embracing political party (the CCM) once ruled supreme, stifling any voice of protest, now there are new political parties with differing opinions. Education has brought awareness—of human rights and gender equality—and an aspiration toward higher standards of living.

Street kids and beggars have increased and are often victims of police brutality. Boys called *wamachinga* (mobile shopkeepers), who are usually migrants from rural areas, move around with heaps of items for sale (kitchenware, clothes, cosmetics), searching for customers.

Accommodation may also be hard to find and afford. Many families live in a single room, with a mattress on the floor as the only furniture, while those who are better off may have a small table and several wooden stools, handwoven mats, and a number of beds and mattresses.

Opposite: **A village woman pounding corn outside her hut.**

The Arusha Conference Center was built when Arusha was used as the capital for the East African Community. It has all the modern facilities, including an interpretation system.

There are richer areas in all towns, of course. Well-fenced, spreading, one-story villas (many of them built in earlier colonial days) form the residences of today's Tanzanian government officials, the wealthier businessmen, and the occasional foreign entrepreneur. An increasing number of German families, who may have ties from the days of German East Africa, are building homes along the coast.

BIRTH AND CHILDHOOD

Childbirth is the one aspect of life in Tanzania where men do not rule supreme. Under rural tradition a special hut was built in which childbearing took place. The women of the extended family move into the hut. The husband might visit, but was not allowed in. If the mother were unable to breastfeed the baby, one of the other women would do so. Today's women do not want the large families of old, and neither do their husbands. Thanks to modern medicine, these days more newborns survive birth. The present birth rate is 35.12 per 1,000 persons.

In thousands of rural families it is still considered the duty of the eldest daughter to look after her younger brothers and sisters, while the eldest son is the one who goes to school. More equal opportunities for boys and girls are slowly beginning to open up. As they grow up, the children will be taught their social responsibilities by their family group. Many children, especially boys (in rural areas) still attend initiation school, but the circumcision that used to be part of the rite is no longer considered obligatory. While boys are taught a trade, girls often grow up with the knowledge that their goal is marriage. "A woman is incomplete without a husband" remains the belief for many.

MARRIAGE

"Arranged marriages" in which the girl has little or no say is customary for many Tanzanian families. The parents start planning their daughter's future quite early, for the system of "bride-wealth" is still very much part of the social tradition. The old logic goes: "My women look after my home, working and planting and cooking. So if a man wishes to take away one of my daughters, he must make up for my loss." In the past a future husband might arrange to pay bride-wealth in the form of local beer, goats, and cattle. Nowadays he is more likely to pay in installments or all in cash. The younger the bride, the higher the price she commands. "If she is very young and a virgin, she is worth a lot of cows" is how Tanzanians used to put it.

A boy carrying his sibling on a cloth sling. Children are often expected to look after their younger siblings in Tanzania.

71

A modern wedding in Tanzania.

Marriage arrangements differ according to local customs. Among the Nyamwezi people, the hopeful husband would give something to the father of the girl he wished to marry. If the father accepted the gift, then the bargaining for the bride-wealth would begin. Once the parents have agreed on a husband, no daughter can refuse. To do so would be an embarrassment to her family and the entire village. She can reject a proposal only with her father's consent.

In some tribes there is usually a time (perhaps two months) before the wedding when the future husband and wife get used to living together. The time comes for the agreed bride-price to be paid. Every male member of the bride's family—uncles, grandfather, and brothers—will get a share of this sum. Females, except for the bride's mother and perhaps grandmother, do not receive a share.

The wedding follows either Christian or Muslim custom. The bride is given presents, usually household items such as utensils for the kitchen, clothes, or money. There may follow a period when the new bride lives with her in-laws, being welcomed and looked after tenderly, but eventually the day will come when the husband and wife start off on their own by creating their own home. Perhaps in the course of living together and having children, they may come to love one another. Even if she is unhappy, the bride may not leave her home to stay with her own parents; the parents must not be seen as contributing toward the failure of the marriage.

As more Tanzanians go to live in towns and more children receive an education, the old customs are weakening or being ignored.

Women working as receptionists at the Mount Meru hotel.

THE ROLE OF WOMEN

The patriarchal father-to-son tradition of most of Africa has left the women in Tanzania invisible. The role of the woman, forever in the field or kitchen, is essential to the economy but apparently has no cash value. For years the majority of urban women have worked on tasks such as food processing and preparation, housekeeping, beer brewing, and petty trade. Only a few have found careers in fields such as nursing, teaching, or secretarial work.

The custom of a prospective husband paying for his wife, the bride-wealth, has not ceased. It may seem close to an insult for a woman to be "sold," but it also brings her respect because it gives her a clear worth. In an attempt to regulate marriage, the 1971 Marriage Act was passed, but the topic of bride-wealth was avoided. The Marriage Act also tried to limit the physical punishment that a husband could inflict on his wife, but

Women selling woven wares at a market in Tanzania.

---

during the parliamentary debate over the law one member of parliament protested, saying, "Beating a wife is similar to providing maintenance to a car. It corrects the problem, at least for some time."

Increasing educational opportunities, however, are helping women realize their dreams and achieve a new place in society. In the cities, in particular, more women tend to be educated and are involved in a variety of activities. To counteract continuing prejudice, 37 seats are allocated to women nominated by the president in the Tanzanian National Assembly.

Centuries of tradition will take a long time to disappear. Some men consider the women who are involved in politics "too independent." In Africa, boys are given priority in matters such as food, education, and attention. It is believed that they will become the ones who will lead and care for households. Only recently have men, particularly the educated ones, started to look for educated wives.

HEALTH

East Africa is not one of the healthiest regions of the world. Malaria (which kills around a million people in Africa every year) is always a threat; bilharzia (picked up from tiny, waterborne worms) is commonly present in the waters of Lake Victoria and in Lake Tanganyika; sleeping sickness, caused by tsetse flies, and river blindness, caused by the blackfly, abound as well. An inoculation program for children exists but it does not reach enough of them. Meanwhile the greatest danger to health is quite simply a lack of proper food. According to the United Nations Children's Fund (UNICEF), half the children in Tanzania are malnourished. Although Tanzania escaped the famines that plagued central Africa for several years, 1997 was a time of bad drought.

There are troubling reports in Tanzania about children accidentally inhaling pesticides while they pick coffee. There is some government control on pesticide use in Tanzania now.

A doctor speaking to an AIDS patient.

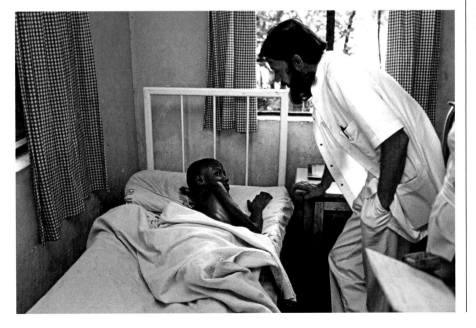

Literacy campaigns have raised Tanzania's level of literacy from 33 percent in 1967 to around 69 percent in 2002.

There is a network of village dispensaries and rural health centers where overworked staffs often have only the simplest medical facilities. Hospitals exist only in the major towns. Statistics indicate that there is a ratio of around one qualified doctor to every 25,000 people. Life expectancy is about 49 years for men and 52 years for women, according to 2007 estimates.

It should be remembered that many Tanzanians do not seek modern medical help. They have greater faith in herbal medicines and traditional healers. In addition, the power of advertising has resulted in speedy sales of what are promoted as "miracle drugs."

THE JOURNEY TOWARD EDUCATION

The people of Tanzania have long realized that reading and writing are the means of obtaining well-paid work. At the turn of the 20th century all education for Africans was in the hands of missionaries, and many of Tanzania's private schools are still run by religious foundations. Primary

AIDS

AIDS has been spreading in many African countries. The AIDS epidemic in Africa has claimed the lives of about 1.6 million people. In some countries, over 10 percent of the population is believed to be HIV-positive. The disease is most common in the urban areas, but it is now spreading into the countryside as well. Tanzania is well aware of the danger of AIDS and has embarked on an effective publicity campaign. By the end of 2007 in sub-Saharan Africa some 22.5 million people were living with HIV, and an estimated 1.6 million people in the region had died from AIDS. It was reported that more than 11 million children were orphaned by AIDS.

education is free, and in 2006 some 8 million pupils were enrolled in 14,700 primary schools. At home, educated members of the extended family are frequently responsible for the education of younger family members. However, less than 8 percent of primary pupils receive secondary schooling. Nearly a million children have either lost parents to the HIV virus or need to take care of sick parents and are not able to go to school. To the youth in Tanzania it seems more important to start working as soon as they can. About 40,000 received technical and higher education at private universities and public universities such as the University of Dar es Salaam or the Sokoine University of Agriculture, Morogoro.

Educators teach lessons in Kiswahili, but the government is also trying to improve English standards for secondary and higher education. All secondary schools are also expected to include practical subjects such as agriculture or bricklaying.

Children studying in a village primary school.

RELIGION

THE MAIN RELIGIONS of Tanzania are Christianity and Islam. The percentage by population is about 30 percent Christian and 35 percent Muslim, including several Muslim sects, although these figures may be misleading because many rural Tanzanians hold on to elements of older religions while also practicing the Islamic or Christian faith. Others have not converted to Christianity or Islam and practice so-called animist faiths. These include forms of ancestor worship and the belief that spirits exist in plants and animals or in places such as volcanoes, mountains, or lakes. Apart from Muslims and Christians, there are also small Asian communities of Hindus and Sikhs.

Many of the country's private schools and medical facilities are attached to mosques and churches. Tanzania claims that there is no religious bias in the country's political and civil administration, but the feeling certainly exists that people who follow traditional faiths instead of one of the accepted world religions are less civilized. Nevertheless, officially, there is freedom of religious worship.

ISLAM

The Arab word *islam* means "to surrender to the will or law of God." Someone who surrenders his life to Islam is called a Muslim. For the millions of Muslims all over the world, Muhammad is the prophet of God (whom they call Allah), who brought the teaching of Islam to the world, as written in the Koran.

Above: **A brightly colored and beautifully designed interior entrance in the Shirazi Mosque.**

Opposite: **The majestic Saint Joseph's Cathedral in Dar es Salaam.**

Islam was brought to the eastern coast of Africa. Tanzania's coastal towns were established by Arabs—therefore, their inhabitants are predominantly Muslim. The islanders of Zanzibar are predominantly Muslim, and the first mosque was built there in A.D. 1107. Since then around 50 other mosques have been built, mainly in Stone Town. Zanzibar also has Muslim courts that deal specifically with laws on marriage, divorce, and inheritance. In 1935 Sheikh Mubarak Ahmed was entrusted with the task of preparing a Kiswahili translation of the Koran from the original Arabic.

Most Muslims dress more conservatively than others—men usually wear a black or white Muslim cap, while women drape their heads with a black veil. In addition to their regular schooling, Muslim children go to Islamic school to learn the Koran in Arabic. They follow the Islamic calendar and observe Muslim festivals such as Eid el-Fitr (the Festival of Fast-Breaking), a joyous three-day celebration.

Many of Tanzania's Asian Muslims belong to the Ismaili sect that is under the spiritual leadership of the Aga Khan. After the end of World War I, Ismaili Muslims established schools, hospitals, dispensaries, and libraries in coastal areas of Tanzania. The Muslim Sunni and Shia sects are represented as well. The different communities keep mostly to themselves, especially when it comes to marrying, although this tradition is changing a bit among the younger people.

MISSIONS AND CHRISTIANITY

Because of the early establishment of Islam along the coast, Christianity in Tanzania had a greater influence inland. Christian and Muslim populations were approximately equal, each accounting for 30 to 40 percent of the population, with the remainder consisting of atheists and practitioners of other faiths and indigenous religions. The Christian population was composed of Roman Catholics, Protestants, Pentecostals, Seventh-Day Adventists, members of the Church of Jesus Christ of Latter-Day Saints (Mormons), and Jehovah's Witnesses.

The earliest Christian missionaries in Tanzania came from the Church Missionary Society. Dr. J. L. Krapf set out from Zanzibar in 1844 with a letter of introduction to Arab governors from Sultan Sayyid: "This letter is written on behalf of Dr. Krapf, a good man who wishes to convert the world to God. Behave well to him, and be everywhere serviceable to him." The letter must have helped, because Krapf, despite the death of his wife and child from malaria, laid the foundations for a number of mission stations.

Above: **The Ismaili Mosque in Zanzibar.**

Opposite: **A Muslim boy holding his Koran. Many Muslim children are sent to Koranic schools in addition to their regular schooling.**

By 1872 Freedom Village of the Catholic Holy Ghost Mission had housed more than 300 children and young adults. The morale boost given to the antislavery movement by the mission could be said to have heralded the beginning of the end for the East African slave trade.

The first Catholic mission established its base in Bagamoyo in 1868, the same year that the Holy Ghost Fathers built what is now known as the Fathers' House. As Christian missionary work moved inland, the London Missionary Society purchased a steamer for work on Lake Tanganyika in 1876. In addition, reacting to an appeal from explorer David Livingstone, the Universities Mission to Central Africa set up its first mission station at

THE MORAVIAN CHURCH

The work of the Moravian church was particularly significant in rural areas. The Moravians taught reading and writing alongside the Christian moral code. Their love of singing and church music made the Moravian missions highly popular. They continue to be centers of activity, often linking several villages together. Services are often colorful and noisy, with an African band playing tunes.

Magila, in the hilly country behind Tanga. From here a number of other mission posts were opened, with schools and hospitals.

After losing their struggle against the colonizing Germans in 1905, many of the Tanzanian tribes abandoned the traditional spirits and magic that they believed had failed to protect them. There were mass conversions to Christianity. The work of the Christian missions, with their churches, schools, and medical clinics, helped establish the ideals of European civilization, although they were often insensitive about respecting local customs. They were regarded as subversive by some as they taught women new ideas about freedom, love, and marriage. One of the traditional customs halted by the arrival of Christianity was that of polygamy, where a man could have several wives. The Christian missions could not stop the way that parents chose husbands for their daughters, but they did allow boys and girls to meet more often in church and school.

TRADITIONAL BELIEFS

The growing strength of Christianity and Islam has not changed the many traditional beliefs that abound in Tanzanian society. Many people continue to hold their belief in spirits or witchcraft alongside their Muslim or Christian beliefs. For example, a string of selected leaves above a doorway is said to keep out evil spirits. Anyone foolish enough to pick one of the white flowers of the baobab tree is certain to be eaten by a lion (because the

Above: **The entrance of the Church of Christ Cathedral in Zanzibar.**

Opposite: **The interior of Saint Joseph's Catholic Cathedral in Stone Town.**

83

The island of Pemba is a popular center for traditional African medicine. People who need to be cured of mental or bodily ailments come from Zanzibar and the mainland of Tanzania— and sometimes even from other countries—to visit Pemba's traditional doctors.

flowers stink like rotting meat, they may even attract lions). Red-rimmed eyes in people are said to be a clear sign of witchcraft (even though most rural families cook over thorn wood and cow-dung, which can make anyone's eyes red). On Zanzibar, parents make sure their children behave by telling them scary tales of the *popobawa*, which is supposed to be a cruel dwarf with one eye and batlike wings. Many adults also claim to have had bones broken by the *popobawa* attacking them in the night. After the disaster on Lake Victoria in which the ferry MV *Bukoba* capsized and sank, relatives of those who drowned followed an ancient ritual. They wove a white shroud, weighted it with rocks, and lowered it into the lake to pacify the watery spirits so that the spirits would not claim other people in the same way.

A traditional healer performs his own dance rituals.

SHOEBOX LIBRARIES

This worthwhile project was launched in Dar es Salaam in 1968, copying the initiative of Joyce Chaplin, founding editor of Africa Christian Press in Ghana. Each cardboard box contains 20 booklets: 10 in Swahili, and 10 in English. The books are mainly about Christianity, but the mini-libraries also include books on topics such as health, nutrition, agriculture, literacy, and raising children. A small deposit is charged to ensure their return. In some areas a reading room is set up in a school or church, and people can sit and read there without charge.

Project Habari in Moshi trains librarians and starts small rural libraries. Sponsored by the Evangelical Lutheran Church in Tanzania, some 50 parish librarians have been trained. Their aim is to ensure that every congregation has a library and a librarian.

Since 1973 Tanzania has maintained a wide network of public libraries, which includes bookmobiles in rural areas. It was halted due to economic reasons such as high fuel and maintenance costs. Tanzania still maintains more than 3,000 village libraries, better classified as reading rooms, with about 400 titles available in each.

The method (as used in magistrates' courts) of swearing on the Bible does not carry the same solemn constraint to tell the truth for traditional-minded Tanzanians as the old tribal oaths did. With the Chaga people, a man may gather a little soil from the ground, put it in his mouth, and say, "If I lie let this earth kill me."

OL DOINYO LENGAI

The Masai consider the active volcano Ol Doinyo Lengai in the Rift Valley to be the "Mountain of God." It is the sacred place of their god, *Ngai* (ung-AI), and his messenger, *Kindong'oi*, from whom the Masai believe their priests are descended. If the peak is not in sight (when the Masai move about with their grazing herds), they will conduct their worship under specially designated fig trees. The Masai pray, particularly at sunrise, for protection from natural evils such as drought and famine.

'iff ya

moja Bonga!

Maongezi Marefu.
Wakati Wowote.

...buna za Malipo ya Awali?
...f antayo inakidhi mahitaji yako. Tariff
...dae kwenda Celtel.

Nzado au, Pamoja au Bonga

...tatua namba 1!   Sh. 1 ni bila VAT.

celtel
Making life better

...ZANIA MUSL..
&
...DRASATUL FAL..

INVITES ALL..

..R'AN ..

..OMPE..

..T & CEN..

1428 A..

BOYS C..
..riday & Saturday, Date 28th, 2..
Venue: Al-Juma Mosq..

GIRLS C..
Friday, Date 28th Sep..
Venue: Starlight..

FINAL R..
Saturday, Date 29th S..
Venue: Diamond Jubilee Ha..

LANGUAGE

THE PROSPERITY AND ADVANCEMENT of the Arab-dominated coastal regions resulted in the Kiswahili (ki-swah-HEE-lee) language of those areas becoming the one used for commerce and government. When the country was German East Africa, Kiswahili was also used as the language for government matters. Today Kiswahili is the country's de facto official language. Although it is spoken as a mother tongue by only about 9 percent of the population, 90 percent of Tanzanians use it as a second language for intertribal communication and official matters.

Some remote rural areas cling to dialects of their own. Tanzania has some 120 different linguistic groups, all of which are confined to specific tribal areas. The Masai, for example, speak their own Masai language, which is totally unlike any other language spoken locally. Masai language is thought to belong to the Nilotic group of languages that originated in

Primary education is done in Kiswahili, although the teenagers who go on to secondary school show an increasing desire to learn English as well.

Left: **Men reading newspapers in the market.**

Opposite: **Advertising posters on a colonnade in Dar es Salaam.**

the Nile Valley. Growth in the private sector and investment has made English more important. It is spoken in the larger towns and popular tourist destinations, and is also used for commerce and government. Many educational institutions, including schools and universities, use English as the medium for instruction.

WHERE DOES LANGUAGE COME FROM?

There seem to be four main root languages in Africa, corresponding with geographical areas: Afro-Asiatic, Niger-Congo, Nilo-Saharan, and Khoisan.

The mother tongue of most Tanzanian children comes from the Niger-Congo region of western Africa. This group of languages is often called *Bantu*, a word that means "the people," coming from the word *ntu*, meaning "man," and the plural prefix *ba-*. The Bantu languages were, of course, spoken languages. The idea of capturing language in writing only came to East Africa through foreign visitors—first the Arabs (who wrote Arabic) and later the European missionaries (who wanted to translate the Bible into the local language).

A door carved with Arabic inscriptions in the House of Wonders in Zanzibar.

KISWAHILI IS BORN

The Arabic word *sawahili* means "of the coast," and was first used to describe the people Arab traders met there. By the 12th century a tribe calling itself the Swahili built towns, forts, and palaces. The demands of trade required easy communication between the Arab traders and the Africans, so the Bantu mother tongue spoken by the Swahili added a mixture of Arabic words. Attempts to capture the language in writing

THE NAME OF THE LANGUAGE

Although it is often referred to as "Swahili," the correct name for the language is *Kiswahili*. The first syllable (prefix), *ki-*, indicates that it is a language. *English* (in Kiswahili) is *Kiingereza* and *French* is *Kifaransa*. In the same way, the prefix *wa-* indicates a group of people, so the speakers of Kiswahili are correctly known as *Waswahili*.

(at first using the Arabic script of the Koran) led to further changes in the language. Under British influence, Kiswahili changed a bit more as writers set it down in the Roman alphabet (which we use for English). The first dictionary of Kiswahili was compiled in 1903.

Kiswahili was originally spoken only by the inhabitants of the eastern coast of Africa. It penetrated westward with the Arab ivory and slave caravans, and is now the main language of Tanzania, Kenya, and Uganda. It is also spoken in many parts of eastern and central Africa. Together with Hausa, it is one of the most widely spoken African languages. When you add up all the Kiswahili-speaking communities around the world, the total comes to nearly 50 million people. Although there are several regional dialects, the purest Kiswahili is supposedly that spoken on Zanzibar, and the Institute of Kiswahili and Foreign Languages is located on the island.

Most Tanzanians talk to one another in Kiswahili, largely because of the efforts of Julius Nyerere to get rid of the remnants of colonial languages such as German and English. In 1974 Nyerere ordered that all titles in Tanzania, including "Mister," should be replaced by *Ndugu*, meaning "brother." By making Kiswahili the national language in 1967, Nyerere was also attempting to unify the country and create a sense of national identity larger than the many ethnic identities.

Children at Uhuru primary school. Kiswahili is the medium of instruction in most primary schools.

HOW DOES THE LANGUAGE FIT TOGETHER?

Our English language uses many suffixes, bits that are added at the end of the word. To make a word plural we usually add the suffix -s—for example, turning *book* into *books*. In Swahili, as with many of the Bantu languages, a prefix (at the beginning of the word) is added instead of a suffix. For example, the prefix *m-* is singular and the prefix *wa-* is plural. So *mtu* means "a person," while *watu* means "people." When a noun in linked with an adjective, both prefixes change. So *mtu mzuri* means "a good person," while *watu wazuri* means "good people." (That *m* at the beginning of a word is pronounced like "hum" without the "hu.")

Here are a few common Swahili words:
aiskrimu (ah-ees-KREE-moo) ice cream
banda (BAN-dah) hut
hoteli (ho-TELL-ee) a local restaurant, not a hotel
mayai (mah-YAH-ee) eggs
wazungu (wah-ZOON-goo) white people

Kiswahili is Romanized, and children learn the rudiments of language using the alphabet that Western children know.

GREETINGS

Jambo (YAM-boh) is the Kiswahili word for "hello" and is used as a general greeting. The greetings *hujambo* (hu-YAM-boh) or *habari* (ha-BAR-ree) both mean "How are you?" or "What's new?"

Many Africans have an elaborate ritual of greeting that they perform before they move on to any further conversation. When two men meet, after the initial *Jambo mzee*, there will be solemn inquiries about the other's health and family, and only then will the men say, "*Habari gani?* (What's new?)." *Mzee* (m-ZEE) is a term of respect, used by younger people when they talk to older people. Another more common term of respect (like "sir" or "mister") is *Bwana* (BWAH-nah), which is a short form that means "the father of many sons." To an older woman, one says "*Bibi.*" In business or polite conversation, Tanzanians often address one another by their last name, using first names only to address members of their family.

In some parts of Tanzania it is considered polite to clap the palms of the hands together when thanking someone or greeting someone who has come from far away. This is also done to mourn someone's death. The threefold African handshake—palm, thumb, palm—is also widely used. (The thumb sign used by hitchhikers in some countries may be considered a rude gesture in Tanzania.)

Two women greeting one another with a clasp of the hands.

PUBLISHING

The oldest publishers in Tanzania were the missionary presses, which printed Bibles and religious pamphlets. Then came the government printers, which, since colonial times, have produced copies of laws, the government gazette, and sometimes official newspapers. The government has also printed textbooks for secondary and higher levels of education. There are also "parastatal" publishing houses such as Tanzania Publishing House, which are joint ventures between the government and overseas firms. Small, private publishers seldom survive unless they manage to get at least one

If you are invited into someone's home, you will be greeted with "Karibuni!" (ka-ree-BOO-nee), meaning "Welcome!"

A woman running a newsstand. It is hard to obtain many of the daily papers outside of Dar es Salaam.

Tanzanian children also read books from abroad. Roald Dahl's popular Charlie and the Chocolate Factory *has been translated into Kiswahili.*

book accepted as a school supplementary reader. Outside the educational field, books and publishing have been considered part of the struggle to "construct a socialist society" and break away from capitalism. In that form, publishing is thriving in Tanzania, although the publications are seldom known outside the urban areas.

Tanzanians read books, it seems, but they seldom *buy* books. Tanzanians connect books with education and therefore expect the books to be provided by the school or college. Many people also do not have the extra money to spend on books, which are expensive. As a result books are mainly seen as luxury items. There are very few bookshops in Dar es Salaam, other than some secondhand bookstalls, and kiosks where international news magazines are popular. There are not many libraries either, although the island of Pemba proudly opened its first-ever public library in 1994. It has about 1,500 regular users, mostly from Chake Chake (Pemba's main town), and it has a book stock of about 13,000 titles. It has many English language works on Zanzibar and Tanzania.

THE MEDIA

Press freedom, but with an obligation to keep political peace, is supported by the government. The Newspaper Act allows the authorities within the government—including the president—the power to prohibit any publication that may not be in the nation's best interest. The news media have been carefully controlled by the government for many years. President Nyerere stated quite openly, "No government likes to be criticized," which was why the main newspapers in Tanzania belonged for a while either to the government or to the main political party. Since the establishment of multiparty politics in 1992, many privately owned newspapers in both English and Kiswahili have appeared, besides the government-owned *Daily News*. Tanzanians have access to 17 newspapers, including two on the Internet.

Tanzania has the state-controlled Radio Tanzania, which airs programs in Kiswahili and English. Television news is aired in Kiswahili. In rural areas with no newspapers, the people rely on radio broadcasts for their news. The government has used radio programs to promote adult literacy and to spread information on better nutrition and ecological conservation.

A Muslim man watching afternoon prayers on television.

THE CHILDREN'S BOOK PROJECT

The Children's Book Project was started in 1991 in response to the acute shortage of books in Tanzania, especially books for children. Supported by the Aga Khan Foundation and international donor organizations in Denmark, the Netherlands, and Canada, the project aims to produce children's books in Kiswahili. These books are distributed to rural libraries, primary schools, and teachers' centers, and some books are sold to bookshops. The project has more than 200 titles published under it and thousands of books distributed free of charge to primary schools, teacher resource centers, and rural libraries in Tanzania. The project also includes courses for writers, publishers, and illustrators.

ARTS

THE IDEA OF AN "ARTIST" was almost unknown in the early ages in Africa. The ancient painters who created the paintings of dancers, giraffes, and buffalo on huge boulders near Dodoma would probably have been thought of as priests or medicine men by their hunter-gatherer people. These boulders are the oldest indigenous art in Tanzania. The painter or carver in Africa was not an individual who created art for his or her own satisfaction. He or she was merely a member of the community who happened to be better at painting or carving than the others, someone who created what was required by the community, yet always with a touch of individuality. African sculpture is closely connected with traditional beliefs in the spirits of ancestors and the conviction that the course of events can be influenced by magical practices.

Alongside the traditional art of the African tribes, other artistic styles also occur in Tanzania, because of the influence of early Arab and Indian traders in the 16th and 17th century. These are reflected particularly in the architecture on the eastern coast.

Left: **A painting of the various animals found on the African safari rides.**

Opposite: **An intricately carved, thick protective door in Stone Town. Zanzibar is known for its beautifully carved doors, many fitted with spikes to prevent elephant attacks, which took place frequently in the past.**

CARVING AND CRAFTWORK

African woodcarvers seldom waste wood on an item that has no practical use. Yet they also lavish great skill on their craft items. A village elder would have a more elaborately carved stool than the plain ones used by many women. A typical traditional throne for a Nyamwezi chief might have a three-legged circular seat with a tall, curved backrest, carved with a suitably imposing human figure. Neck supports and combs were important to allow people to sleep without messing up their hair, since in tribes such as the Masai, the men spend an enormous amount of time arranging their headdress. Arab chests from Zanzibar with elaborately carved details indicate the wealth that might be locked inside.

Masks were created for specific dances on occasions such as the initiation into adult life or a ritual to bring rain or increase crops. For these masks, the carved faces might represent dead ancestors or their spirits. Other masks were carved to scare away evil spirits or to increase fertility so that the tribe would become numerous and strong.

A woodcarver at work. The elaborate carvings on personal items such as a stool or headrest make the owner more admirable in the eyes of his or her peers.

DAILY ITEMS

Whether the countless objects made for everyday use—baskets, pottery, mats, metalwork, jewels, and beads—should be classified as craftwork or art is debatable. Most are made to earn some quick money; a few are made with style and skill. Beads are used extensively by Tanzanians for

MAKONDE

According to legend, the first carver lived alone in the forest. There he shaped a piece of wood into a female likeness and left it outside his hut overnight. In the morning he found that the carving had come alive and was now a beautiful woman. The child she had with the carver was the first true Makonde.

Perhaps the most famous wood sculptors in Africa, the Makonde have been carving for at least 300 years. They came originally from northern Mozambique and now live in the southeastern part of Tanzania on the Makonde Plateau, which is relatively isolated. They have built villages of woodcarving workshops, where they sell their crafts to tourists or curio dealers. They carve face masks, figures, and drums. They carve figures of ghosts and spirits from the legends of their people. The human faces that they carve are gaunt and are intricately decorated with geometrical tattooing. Male masks are bearded, sometimes with human hair; female masks may have a disk-shaped peg set in the upper lip. Modern styles have become more imaginative and abstract. Some carvings, called *Shetani*, portray devil figures and flesh-eating monsters based on Makonde folklore.

Today among some of Tanzania's noted artists is Kiure Msangi, who makes delicate lino prints. It is a technique of overprinting with three colors where each color is allowed to come prominently through the other colors. The black lines are the last color printed. Another noteworthy artist is Eduardo S. Tingatinga, who established an art form that is associated with Tanzania and named after him.

Palm leaves being woven into mats.

bodily adornment. Originally they were made from the shell of ostrich eggs. Then came glass or ceramic beads imported from other places, but the skill of arranging them and the distinctive patterns are still African. Other handicrafts include mats or baskets woven from young palm fronds or dried banana leaves. Pots are both decorative in the home and useful, because many Tanzanian housewives prefer to cook in clay pots rather than metal ones.

LITERATURE

The oral (spoken) literature of East Africa is endless and includes proverbs and riddles, myths and legends, and interwoven songs and dances. Storytelling remains a skill of which many Tanzanian mothers are proud—and it has not been replaced by television. The first-known written work in the Tanzanian region was written in about 1520. It was in Arabic and was about the history of the city-state of Kilwa Kisiwani. This was followed by histories of other cities written in an early form of

Kiswahili. In 1728 the epic Kiswahili poem *Utendi wa Tambuka* (*The Story of Tambuka*) started a steady stream of story verse with Arab themes that were romantically flavored for East African readers. A Kiswahili novel by James Mbotela, *Uhuru wa Watumwa* (*Freedom of the Slaves*), was published in 1934, but it was the writing of Tanzanian poet Shaaban Robert in the 1950s and 1960s that gained genuine respect for Kiswahili literature.

President Julius Nyerere was also a respected author and translator. His work *Education for Self-Reliance* set out his theories on a suitable education system. Appreciative of culture, he also translated two plays of Shakespeare into Kiswahili—*Julius Caesar* and *The Merchant of Venice* (which, in his translation, he called *The Capitalist of Venice*).

LITTLE GRANNY

Fatuma Bintibaraka from Zanzibar is known affectionately as Little Granny (she is over 93). For many years (in the 1920s and 1930s) the Zanzibaris heard her lilting voice but never saw her face, for Islamic women were required to cover themselves from head to toe when they went out in public. She learned all her songs from Siti Binti Saad, the first woman singer in Zanzibar, and she sings in both Arabic and Swahili.

Fatuma (now simply known as *Bi Kidude*) became famous outside Tanzania. In the 1980s she toured Germany, Japan, the Persian Gulf, Paris, and London with a *taarab* band (traditional music from Egypt, played with fiddles, flutes, drums and rattles, and singing). While on this tour she lifted her veil. She plays with the Shikamoo Jazz Band, veteran musicians who raise money for the elderly in Tanzania. This is her personal *uhuru*, an adventurous journey of freedom. At the 2005 World Music Expo (WOMEX), Bi Kidude received an award for her lifetime achievements and contributions to world music. A documentary film about her, called *As Old as My Tongue—The Myth and Life of Bi Kidude*, was recently made.

Two German missionaries Johannes Rebmann and Ludwig Krapf spotted the snow-capped Mount Kilimanjaro in 1848 and initiated hot debates across Europe. Their tales about a snow-covered peak near the equator were not initially believed until 1889 when Hans Meyer, a German geographer from Leipzig University climbed to the top of Mount Kilimanjaro and witnessed the snow.

MUSIC AND DANCING

In his first year as president, Julius Nyerere set up a Ministry of National Culture to encourage a wider appreciation of indigenous art forms. He was particularly concerned about the way native dancing was being forgotten. He said, "But how many of us can or have even heard of *Gombe Sugu*, the *Mangala*, the *Konge, Nyang'umuni, Kiduo* or *Lele mama*?"—all names of Tanzanian dances. In due course, groups of university students were encouraged to take traditional dance classes, and Tanzania's newly formed National Dancing Troupe soon toured the country, learning and performing dances from all the regions.

Music and dance are part of the same process, because the musician moves his body and limbs during the process of making music. (It is virtually impossible to capture true African music in musical notation on paper.) Sometimes everybody who is present takes part in the music; sometimes musical specialists lead the music or dance routine, or perform on their own. Many traditional dances feature masked dancers, often performing in pairs. The masks may represent animals, devil spirits, or ancestral spirit powers. Dancers may also use body paint or costumes, rattling gourds, and strings of beads, and they may hold spears or marimbas. Singing is a way of communicating. Often songs have a "call and response" pattern. In the same way that words in African dialects can change meaning according to the intonation and pitch of the voice, so does sung music tend to follow the setting and rhythm of the words.

Drumming, dancing, and songs are often part of special ceremonies. They may celebrate the initiation of youths who have been accepted as men, or they may try to please the spirits of the ancestors or drive away evil spirits that might affect the fertility of the tribe or their cattle. Drums

The impressive House of Wonders Palace built for Sultan Barghash in 1883 preserves some of the most striking Zanzibar doors under the shade of wide verandas.

A Makonde man playing a tambusa drum.

help hold a rhythm or build up tension, and are nearly always used. There are many different types of drums. Some are pointed at one end so that they can be firmly bedded in the ground, some have their own legs or supports, and some are held between the knees.

Another percussion instrument is the xylophone, which makes use of the resonant qualities of different woods. Hand clapping and foot stamping are also popular. Tanzanian music uses stringed instruments with resonators (such as a coconut shell or gourd) and pipes made of bamboo or animal horns.

All these instruments have their roots in traditional music, but they are also used to create modern swing and jive music. In addition, what might once have been solemn chanting and hymns in local churches have instead been livened up by the pleasure that many Tanzanians take in choral singing.

ARCHITECTURE

There is no memorable house-building style that is peculiar to Tanzania, probably because of a lack of permanent materials,

A modern update of the traditional village house that used to be made from mud and poles.

combined with the fact that the people may be nomadic or create only small settlements. The use of natural materials (wood, mud, twigs, thatch) results in impermanent structures that rot in the heat and humidity. Poles from mangrove trees are still used for building because the wood is resistant to termites. More permanent architectural styles in Tanzania have arrived with settlers or colonizers: Islamic mosques, Indian carved doors, Bavarian buildings, and British colonial hotels in Dar es Salaam, as well as uninspired modern apartment and office blocks.

On the island of Zanzibar, however, buildings have a particularly distinctive feature. It became the custom to build the doorway of a house before the house itself—because the entrance was considered the key to the well-being of the building. Solid square teak frames were installed, often with texts from Koran decoratively carved on them to increase the good fortune of the people who dwelled within. Under later Indian influences, doors with arched tops and more elaborate designs were introduced. Motifs with specific meanings were carved among geometrical and floral designs. Chains represented security, the precious frankincense tree stood for riches, shoals of fish encouraged fertility, and the sacred lotus flower was a symbol of reproductive power.

Sadly the historic buildings of Zanzibar have suffered from neglect and decay. So it is heartening to see benefactors such as the Aga Khan (the spiritual leader of the Ismaili Muslims) sponsoring building restoration, while a number of other structures are being preserved by selling them to private owners.

The 1894 Dispensary in Zanzibar was restored by the Aga Khan Trust for Culture and now serves as the Stone Town Cultural Center.

LEISURE

WHAT IS "LEISURE" when you work all day to grow enough food to survive? Perhaps it is listening to the radio when it is too dark to work any more. Or maybe it is the chance to sing and worship and meet your friends at church on Sunday. Whether the reason is a joyous wedding or a sad funeral, a meeting of the "extended family" is given high priority in Tanzania. People will travel great distances for special occasions despite the problems with the Tanzanian transportation system.

Tanzanians love music and dancing, so the village *ngoma* (un-GOH-mah), or dance, for different social occasions is welcomed by all. There may be a live band with some traditional dancing or perhaps someone will have a tape of a popular Zairean rock group. There are discos in most towns now as well as villages, even if they just play scratchy disks on a battery-operated record player. Movies are a favorite leisure activity. There is one multiplex cinema in Dar es Salaam, and the popular taste is for action features involving war, gangsters, and kung-fu fighting.

RELAXING

On most evenings the older folk will sit and talk, often with the men and women sitting separately. In towns the men will sit along a bar with a few bottles of Safari Lager (unless they are Muslims for whom alcohol is prohibited). In the villages there will be an evening of drinking

Above: **A modern woman sings at a club in Dar es Salaam.**

Opposite: **Men playing checkers in Dar es Salaam.**

105

homemade beer under the spreading branches of a tree. If it is a hot night and the young ones cannot sleep, their grandmother may keep alive the old custom of storytelling with some folktale about giants, cannibals, or talking animals.

BAO

Bao is a traditional African game (similar to the *kigogo* played in Kenya). It is played using a wooden board with parallel rows of holes, or just hollows scooped out of the sand. The two players have pieces (beans or pebbles) that they aim to place in such a way that will "capture" their opponent's pieces. The rules are complicated and tend to be different from region to region.

CHILDREN'S GAMES

Children play make-believe games in Tanzania, as they do everywhere. However, they are also required to help with the domestic chores. Some children help one another fetch water or weed vegetables, so that there is time for them all to play later. The boys enact war games and fake fights. The girls hold play weddings, using dolls made from scraps of cloth and fiber with black thread for hair. The bride-wealth is arranged and paid, and perhaps a make-believe cow is killed for the feast. With much drumming and dancing, the two dolls are placed side by side in bed.

Another favorite game is called the Monkey Game, which is much like hide-and-seek, where one child is "it" and stays by the goal while the others run and hide. They call out, "Oh, ooh, ay!" and the one who is "it" goes to look for them. Any child who is touched and caught must go and wait by the goal (like a tied-up monkey) until everyone has been caught.

Boys playing soccer at a beach. Soccer is the favorite sport of young Tanzanians.

SPORTS

Soccer is the favorite sport in Tanzania, whether it is played or just watched and shouted about. In the smallest villages, boys will kick around a ball made of rags if they don't have a real one. Crowds will go to support their favorite local teams in the larger towns. The first time Zanzibar won a competition since the East and Central African Senior Challenge Cup started in 1947 was on December 9, 1995, when it beat Uganda 1–0 in the final. As a reward, each player received a motorcycle from Zanzibari President Salmin Amour. In addition, the goalie (Rifat Said) and the player who scored the winning goal (Victor Bambo) received 1 million Tanzanian shillings each from the delighted president. All of Tanzania was wildly excited. In 2007 the national team, the Taifa Stars, came close to qualifying for the CAF African Cup of Nations Ghana 2008. The "Win in Africa with Africa" soccer management program, launched in 2006, is a timely intervention as Tanzania prepares to launch into full-time professional soccer.

Volleyball is becoming a popular game for men and women, and the new seaside variation of beach ball is starting to catch on. A few people also go to watch boxing or wrestling matches. Otherwise, apart from women's netball and a game of darts in the bar for the men, Tanzanians do not play many structured sports.

TANZANIA SCOUTS ASSOCIATION

The Boy Scout movement in Tanzania was founded in 1919 and now has more than 90,000 members. Scouts (and Girl Guides) of Tanzania follow the same sort of self-reliance programs that lay behind the *ujamaa* villages. Tanzanian Scouts are far more active in community service than are the Scouts in some other countries. In the spirit of the universal Boy Scout motto, *Uwe tayari* (OO-wee TAY-AR-EE), "Be prepared," they "learn by

Children also play the Blindfold Game, where all the children are covered up with a blanket, except for one. That one has to feel the others through the blanket until she or he recognizes one and calls out the child's name.

MARATHON

Tanzanian sportsmen have excelled in long-distance running. In 1978 Gidamis Shahanga was the first black African to win the Commonwealth Games marathon in Alberta, Canada. In 1980, at the Moscow Olympics, Tanzanian Suleiman Nyambui won a silver medal in the 5,000-meter marathon and Filbert Bayi won the silver in the 3,000-meter steeplechase. In 1984 Juma Ikangaa came in sixth in the marathon in the Los Angeles Olympics, but in September 1986, he won the Tokyo marathon, completing it in 2 hours, 8 minutes, 10 seconds, which was the tenth-fastest time in the history of the marathon. Then, in 1989, the amazing Juma Ikangaa won the New York marathon in 1989 with a new record time of 2 hours, 8 minutes, 1 second. Tanzania won its first-ever team competition with a cumulative time of 3 hours, 3 minutes, 1 second in the World Half Marathon Championships in 2003.

doing" in connection with many health and conservation projects. For example, in 1994, the Tanzania Scouts Association launched a campaign to publicize health knowledge (in collaboration with UNICEF and the Ministry of Health). Scouts traveled door-to-door demonstrating to mothers how to prepare oral rehydration salts. They explained the benefits of oral rehydration salts, which contain a combination of electrolytes and sugar that stimulates water and electrolyte absorption and helps prevent diarrhea. They reinforced the message with puppet shows and plays. More recently Scouts have worked in refugee camps, building shelters and helping to feed malnourished children.

A man playing golf at a range in Tanzania.

WEALTHIER INDULGENCES

Some Tanzanians visit the game parks, where they pay a much lower tariff (a schedule of charges imposed by the government for a public utility) for entry, guides, and accommodation than overseas visitors. It is possible to book a camel safari across the Serengeti or even to indulge in a balloon ride above the wildlife parks, enjoying a champagne breakfast after the flight. Around the country there are also facilities for playing tennis or golf.

Riding over the Serengeti in a hot-air balloon. The balloon is dully colored to avoid startling the animals.

FESTIVALS

IN THE COUNTRYSIDE the pattern of life is mostly adjusted to fit in with religious festivals. These tend to be the Christian holidays in inland Tanzania. The people of the coastal towns are mostly Muslim, so they celebrate Islamic festivals such as Eid el-Fitr and the Prophet Muhammad's birthday, along with political holidays. In addition, people participate in important events related to the life cycle, such as weddings, coming-of-age rites, and funerals. Some have maintained traditional customs, while others have been replaced, often by Christian customs. The majority of Tanzanian people make their living by growing crops or tending animals, so festivities have to accommodate chores as well. Cows waiting to be milked cannot be ignored just because the day is officially a public holiday.

Left: **Young Makua boys receive money on their initiation day.**

Opposite: **Women dancing during the Islamic New Year festival in Tanzania.**

NATIONAL HOLIDAYS

New Year's Day has been a holiday almost everywhere in the world for well over 2,000 years. In Tanzania people wait for the church bells to ring at midnight, and then good luck toasts are drunk for the new year ahead. January 1 is a public holiday.

On January 12 the people of Zanzibar celebrate their own independence, which was achieved in the Revolution of 1964.

In February the dominant CCM party waves its banners and makes political promises during a day of parades and speeches called Chama Cha Mapinduzi Day. Then in April come the festivities of Union Day in recognition of the merging of Tanganyika and Zanzibar into the United Republic of Tanzania on April 26, 1964. Most schools prepare special celebrations for this day. More political rallies and processions, particularly on behalf of the workers and the poorer people, take place on May Day (May 1) and Peasants' Day (August 8). No longer a celebration of country customs, May Day (or Labor Day) around the world has become linked with industrial achievements and trade unions. Unions are now legal in Tanzania, although they were forbidden for a long time.

Independence Day on December 9 is another grand public holiday like Union Day, celebrating Tanzania's independence from Great Britain in 1961. With Christmas in sight and the schools on holiday, this is a chance for parties and processions, festivities, and fireworks.

PUBLIC HOLIDAYS**

January 1	New Year's Day
January 12	Zanzibar Revolution Day
March 20	Maulid Day*
April 7	Karume Memorial Day
April 10	Good Friday**
April 12	Easter Monday**
April 26	Union Day
May 1	Workers' Day
July 7	Saba Saba Day
August 8	Peasants' Day
October 2	Eid-el-Fitr*
October 3	Eid-el-Fitr*
October 14	Nyerere Memorial Day
December 9	Independence Day / Eid-el-Hajj*
December 25	Christmas Day
December 26	Boxing Day

*Based on the Islamic lunar calendar
**Based on the calendar year 2009

A Christian minister blessing a baby during a dedication service in Tanga.

NATIONAL ANTHEM

The Tanzanian National Anthem is "*Mungu Ibariki Afrika*" (God Bless Africa), which has essentially the same tune and words as "*Nkosi Sikelel'i Afrika*," chosen by the African National Congress (ANC) as the anthem for the newly democratic South Africa. It is also used as the national anthem for Zambia, Namibia, and Zimbabwe. The words were written in 1867 by Enoch Sontonga, a teacher at a Methodist mission school in South Africa.

CHRISTIAN OBSERVANCES

The two greatest festivals of the Christian year are Christmas, a celebration of the birth of Jesus, and Easter, when Christians believe Jesus rose from the dead after having been crucified. These are colorful celebrations whether they are held in the cities or in the villages.

CHRISTMAS Centered as it is around a newborn baby, Christmas has always been a happy festival for children. In Christian Tanzanian homes, families give whatever presents they can afford, particularly new clothes, to the children. Everyone attends the morning service in church where the children sing the carols they have practiced ("Silent Night" is often one of them). Afterward there is usually some kind of local celebration. In a village this might be a communal meal for church members at someone's house, while in town, there may be dances or sports events that have taken weeks of planning.

EASTERTIDE Eastertide is celebrated a week after Palm Sunday, when palm-waving processions to churches in Tanzania recall the triumphal entry Jesus made to Jerusalem.

Good Friday is associated with the solemn memory of the Crucifixion, a day that makes the joyful singing on Easter Sunday even happier. The European custom of giving Easter eggs has been adopted by some Tanzanians who cannot afford to give boxes of expensive chocolate.

Muslim women in Tanzania carrying their praying mats after performing special Eid el-Fitr prayers to mark the end of the fasting month in Dar es Salaam.

The Ismaili Jama'at Khana (in Dar es Salaam) is a religious center for Ismaili Muslims. During Islamic festivals or on Aga Khan's birthday, it is lit up with strings of colored lights.

MUSLIM FESTIVALS

The festivals of Islam are timed according to local sightings of various phases of the moon, so they fall on different days each year. The tradition of giving food, clothes, and money to the poor is an important part of all Islamic festivals.

RAMADAN During the month of Ramadan all adult Muslims fast from sunrise to sunset and eat only at night. *Iftar* is the first meal that a Muslim eats after a day's fasting The word means "breakfast" in its original sense: to break one's fast. The Prophet Muhammad broke his fast with a few dates soaked in milk, so a typical *iftar* includes dates or sweet fruit juice. Many restaurants in the Muslim parts of Tanzania are closed in the daytime during Ramadan, and normal business takes a backseat.

EID EL-FITR This festival falls at the end of Ramadan. Tanzanian Muslim children enjoy helping their mother cook the sweet biscuits known as *kahk* to eat and to give to the poor. The Prophet Muhammad celebrated the

end of the fasting month by putting on his best clothes, giving charity to the poor, and going to the mosque. All Muslims, therefore, continue that custom.

In Zanzibar, on Eid el-Fitr, people have a custom of their own. The men from south of town challenge those from the north to a contest of fighting with banana branches. When the men are sufficiently bruised and exhausted, the women sing traditional folk songs, and the whole town then eats and dances until late into the night.

THE PROPHET'S BIRTHDAY On the birthday of the Prophet Muhammad, Moulid el-Nabi, there are special services with recitations from the Koran. To show how sweet its words are, the children are given boxes of candy made from nuts.

FAMILY CELEBRATIONS

The influence of the mission churches has stopped many of Tanzania's traditional, family-based ceremonies. Weddings and funerals now take place in church. Baptisms may occur inside or outside in a river. Even those who do not go to church are beginning to forget the old ways.

For a wedding a fresh kanga, *or robe, is essential. Young girls are often given their first* kanga *to mark the beginning of puberty.*

119

The traditional custom of funeral dances has lasted longer. Even after a church funeral, mourners in the family feel the need to join together in a common expression of sadness. The insistent rhythm of the drums gets people dancing silently and solemnly. Children may dance in small groups of their own. All the time the drums keep their beat, broken occasionally by groups of wind instruments wailing in a way that sounds like crying.

TRIBAL RITUALS

MASAI The time when a boy "becomes a man" is exciting in any culture in the world. The people of Africa have their own customs and celebrations, which often involves an initiation test for the young person to prove his manhood. The arrival of Western ways, first through missionaries and then through urbanization, has affected many of these customs in Tanzania, but very little seems to have changed for the Masai.

When a boy is only four or five years old, he may have two teeth removed from his lower jaw. This custom came about because of the danger (in a totally outdoor life) of contracting tetanus from an infected cut. In a case of bad infection, the neck and jaw muscles tighten in a condition known as lockjaw, but a child with a gap in the teeth can still be fed.

When he is about six, the boy has his earlobes pierced so he can wear distinctive bone or metal earrings. At the onset of puberty, he and others of his age receive special instruction and then go through an initiation through circumcision. Although the operation is conducted without anesthetic, the boy is expected to make no sound. Instead, his mother and relatives wail and yell for the pain he is enduring. This is the time of the *emanyatta* feast to celebrate the boys' "coming of age." A fattened bull is killed and its throat slit. The blood is mixed with milk and sipped by everyone present to share its strength. The government tried to ban this ritual in 1973, but the decree was never enforced.

Now the boy is ready to become a *moran* (one of the young warriors who are responsible for protecting the Masai cattle from thieves and wild beasts). He may carry black patterns on his shield of buffalo (or giraffe) hide and plait his hair in elaborate pigtails. To be chosen leader of the *moran*, he must first prove himself as an accepted judge within their group.

At the age of about 20, he becomes a senior warrior. Not until then is he allowed to paint red ochre on his shield and perhaps be given the honor of wearing a lion-mane headdress. The right to wear this headdress was traditionally earned by the *moran* who took the main impact of a lion's charge during a hunt or the one who made the fatal thrust. Now that lion hunting is forbidden, some Masai groups award the right to wear the lion-mane headdress to the warrior they consider the bravest.

The next stage of life is to be admitted as a junior elder, a *moruo*, when he is allowed to marry. If he is chosen later to join the ranks of the senior elders, he is one of those who make all major decisions and will be revered by the whole community.

When he dies, his body will be placed in the bush to be eaten by wild animals. Only the most distinguished elders and those considered Masai prophets (*loibon*) are buried. Today's Masai warriors are not permitted to kill lions and raid cattle. They continue to survive as an icon through their photogenic qualities. No tourist is allowed to take a Masai's picture without paying a fee.

MAKONDE During the dry season of the year (between June and October), curious things start happening in the Makonde villages. A farewell ceremony will be held for a number of men who have announced that they must "go away."

Their village meanwhile prepares for the *Midimu* (me-DEE-mu), which may be a celebration of a large harvest or new fields being planted for the first time, or the end of the period of initiation instruction for the boys and girls. Everyone waits eagerly for the night when, under a waxing moon, masked and therefore unrecognizable dancers come bounding out of the darkness with drums throbbing and lighted torches waving. All the villagers come out of their houses to join them. This is the beginning of a feast that continues for three days and nights.

Eventually the "missing men," all of whom are professional dancers and musicians, return home. Everyone knows why they have been away, but nothing is ever said. Behind their Midimu masks, they were unrecognizable while dancing, as if they were invisible.

FOOD

TAPPING A MIXTURE of African, Indian, and Arab influences, the better Tanzanian cooks combine foods in unusual ways. Their staple foods are the same kinds eaten elsewhere in Africa—corn, cassava, rice, plantains, beans, and okra, as well as coconuts and (depending on the region and the price) beef, chicken, goat meat, or seafood. There is a wide variety of fruit available, including papayas, mangoes, bananas, pineapples, and watermelon.

In many Tanzanian homes, breakfast is a simple spread of bread and butter, although some enjoy a kind of deep-fried doughnut, called *mandazi*, which goes well with their sweet tea. Lunch is usually the main meal of the day: a solid serving of something starchy, such as a porridge called *ugali* (oo-GAH-lee), cassava, or rice, served with beans, pumpkin, or *mchicha*, spinach, with perhaps a small helping of grilled beef or fish. The evening meal is usually light.

The basic aim of most Tanzanian food is to be as filling and as cheap as possible. Meat, which is expensive, is often used just as a flavoring, rather than as a main ingredient.

Left: **A market scene in Zanzibar.**

Opposite: **A man serving food in a restaurant in Dar es Salaam.**

123

UGALI

Ugali (oo-GAH-lee) is a stiff porridge, usually made of corn, and is the main ingredient of the menu for 90 percent of Tanzanians. Because it is not expensive, people can usually afford something to go with it (meat, beans, or spinach), and so they can be sure of one satisfying and fairly balanced meal each day. The housewife starts with the raw grain and pounds it in a mortar before making it into a thick paste with a little water. Then it is added to a large pot of boiling water and boiled until it thickens to form a thick dough. The cook needs a strong arm and a sturdy spoon at this stage. The cooked *ugali* can be eaten hot, or may be left to cool and then cut into slices and fried. Another method is to make holes in the warm *ugali* with a small ladle and fill these with soup or meat. That way both stay warm longer.

MAKING UGALI

1¾ pints (1 liter) of water, or water and milk to make it creamier
2 ounces (55 g) butter or margarine
1 pound (450 g) corn flour
Salt

Mix half the flour and about a quarter of the water in a bowl with a wooden spoon until it is a smooth paste. Boil the rest of the water with the butter and a pinch of salt, and then add the paste, stirring steadily for at least a minute and bringing it back to a boil. Then add the rest of the flour a little at a time while you keep stirring. You will understand how strong Tanzanian cooks must be! Keep stirring until the mixture has turned into a stiff dough. (You can add a little more flour or water if necessary. The mixture should not stick to the pot.)

Although it is usually made from corn, *ugali* can also be made from cassava, millet, or sorghum.

BANANAS

There are at least 17 different varieties of bananas in Tanzania, and probably up to 170 different ways to cook them. They are usually eaten for the evening meal. In addition, there are the larger, slightly tougher, bananalike plantains. Menus can include banana soup, roast bananas served on banana leaves, banana and coconut stew, fried banana chips (which are more popular than potatoes), banana cream as dessert, or fried banana fritters. People also like to drink banana wine, which is sipped through grass straws. In addition to feasting on assorted bananas, the Tanzanians use banana leaves to thatch their homes or as inexpensive umbrellas.

Different regions have their own banana specialties. The creamy banana (or plantain) soup known as *mtory* (um-TOR-ee) is fed to nursing mothers

A tourist commented that the hotel at Jambiani Beach on Zanzibar was "one of those places where the manager comes to you, asks what you want for dinner, and then goes out and catches it."

125

(and to their husbands when no one is looking!) in the Kilimanjaro region. It is made from beef and bones, green bananas or plantains, with onion and tomato.

VILLAGE COOKING

The village housewife manages without an electric oven or a refrigerator. Yet on a paraffin stove or a simple fire of wood and charcoal, she can create cakes, buns, doughnuts, flat cakes, rice-flour bread, stews, meatballs and, of course, *ugali*. Fruit and vegetables come fresh from the vegetable patch or the market. Cassava and *mchicha* are common vegetables. *Mchicha* (spinach) is eaten by everyone in Tanzania because it is cheap and grows everywhere, including backyards. When they can afford it Tanzanians either smoke or dry freshly caught or killed meat and fish. For a rare feast, *ndayu* (un-DAY-oo), a roasted young goat, is a popular delicacy throughout the country.

A simple family meal in the village.

The housewife's utensils include a mortar and pestle, plastic water containers, some bowls and jugs, a tin sheet for bread or biscuits, and cooking pots made of both aluminum and clay because Tanzanian women believe that certain foods taste better when cooked in clay pots, while tea tastes better when prepared in aluminum pots. Many households don't bother with knives and forks; people use their fingers to eat, along with a spoon when necessary.

Smoking meat is a lengthy procedure. The traditional method is to dig a deep pit in the ground and then lay felled trees in it, with their leafy branches spread out in thick layers. The meat is cut lengthwise, washed and salted, then laid neatly on the leaves. The fire is lit and the smoke cures the meat, while at least one person keeps a careful watch to make sure that the fire does not flare too much and scorch the meat.

COASTAL FOOD

Those who are fortunate enough to live beside the Indian Ocean or on the shores of one of the Great Lakes may be able to add varieties of fish or seafood to their diet. On Lake Tanganyika fishermen go out at night with lights hung from the prow of their boats, which attracts the small, sardinelike fish known as *dagaa* (da-GAH) to the surface. A sudden beating of drums scares the fish into momentary stillness before nets scoop them up. Fried when fresh or dried in the sun, these fish form a tasty source of protein. In Lake Victoria lives the large Nile perch. The ocean is also rich in lobsters, crabs, kingfish, and other creatures. Even the poorest people can gather crabs or clams when the tide goes out, boil them in a pot with peeled cassava, and have a tasty meal. Prawns are popularly served hot and spicy, flavored with garlic. Restaurants serve a famous coconut-and-fish curry called *samaki wa nazi* (sah-MAH-kee wah NAH-zee).

DRINKS

The most common drink in Tanzania is tea, although the people have their own special way of making it. Tea leaves and sugar are boiled together,

A seafood vendor by the waterside.

127

A woman stirring a tub of local beer, known as *pombe*. This beer is home-brewed from a variety of grains, often millet. Brewing is a skilled task usually undertaken by women.

sometimes with the addition of cardamom seeds or ginger, and the result is called *chai* (CHAH-ee). Tanzanians drink it with or without milk. Curiously, although they grow and export excellent coffee, Tanzanians do not drink much of it themselves. For visitors, it is usually served black and sprinkled with ginger powder.

Coconut milk is available fresh and drunk with relish, but fruit juices (in a land of cheap fruit) are seldom consumed, possibly because making juice would involve discarding the wholesome flesh of the fruit.

Those who want an alcoholic drink have the choice of beer or *konyagi* (kon-YAH-gee), which is a liquor made from sugarcane. Bottled beer is likely to be Safari or Pilsner; home-brewed beer is called *pombe* (POM-beh). Imported beers from the nearest bordering countries (Kenya, Malawi, and Zaire) are also popular.

EATING OUT

There are countless small town restaurants called *hoteli* (ho-TELL-ee) that usually serve some sort of stew based on rice, or *ugali*, or boiled plantain, together with chicken, beef, goat, or simply a mixture of beans. Food stalls in the street sell *mishkaki* (mish-KAH-ki), which are kebabs of goat or stringy beef, barbecued chicken, triangular spicy samosas, and very hot chili bites called *bhajia* (bah-GEE-ah). When the British arrived in Tanzania, so did the idea of chips. Today potatoes are fried everywhere and passersby can feast on *chipsi na mayai* (chips and egg) or *chipsi na kuku* (chips and chicken).

Tanzanians delight in having dabaga *sauce, a fiery chili sauce produced in Dabaga, near Iringa.*

A cook preparing *mishkaki*, or kebabs, in a wayside store in Tanzania.

129

ZANZIBAR CHICKEN

3 pounds (1.4 kg) chicken thighs or drumsticks
2 teaspoon (10 ml) cinnamon powder
Salt and pepper
2 tablespoons (30 ml) vegetable oil
1 onion (diced)
1 clove garlic (chopped)
¾ cup (180 ml) orange juice
3 tablespoons (45 ml) raisins
⅓ cup (85 ml) slivered almonds

Season the chicken pieces with cinnamon powder, salt, and pepper. Heat oil in a skillet over medium-high heat. Add chicken, in batches if necessary. Fry chicken until brown (about 10 minutes). Remove chicken and set aside. Add diced onion to the pan. Cook until soft (about 3 minutes). Add garlic and cook 1 minute longer. Return the chicken to the skillet. Add orange juice and raisins. Cover, reduce heat, and simmer for 15 minutes or until the chicken is tender. Dish onto a plate and garnish with slivered almonds.

FRUITS OF AFRICA PIE

One cooked, 9-inch pie shell

2 cups (approximately 500 ml) diced fresh fruit (papaya, pineapple, melon, orange, or guava)
  Papaya, guava, or apricot nectar

4 tablespoons (60 ml) cornstarch

4 tablespoons (60 ml) sugar

4 tablespoons (60 ml) lemon juice

1 cup (250 ml) whipped cream

½ cup (125 ml) shredded coconut fresh

½ cup (125 ml) chopped peanuts

Pour ½ cup of papaya, guava, or apricot nectar into a 2-quart saucepan and bring to a boil. Dissolve the cornstarch in the lemon juice. Pour the contents into the nectar and cook until thick and clear. Cool slightly. Add diced fresh fruit, singly or in combination. Cool to room temperature. Pour into pie shell. Chill. Spread whipped cream with sugar over fruit. Sprinkle shredded coconut and peanuts on top.

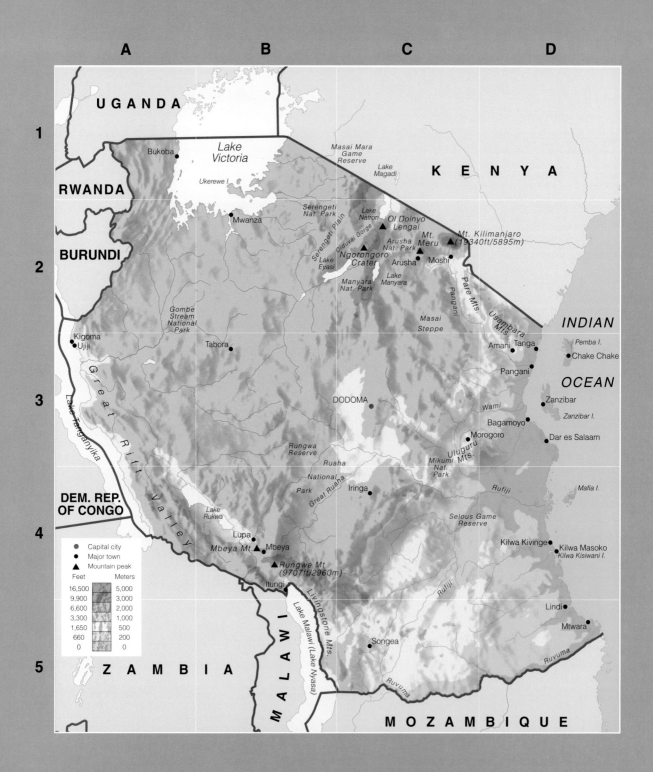

MAP OF TANZANIA

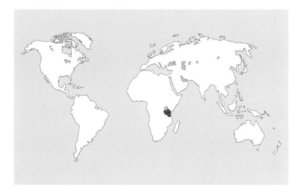

ECONOMIC TANZANIA

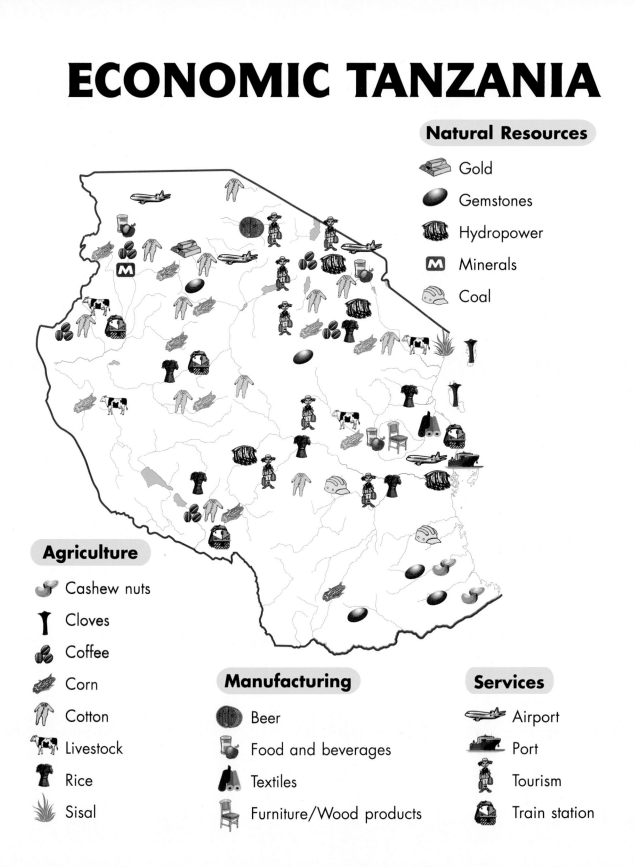

Natural Resources
- Gold
- Gemstones
- Hydropower
- M Minerals
- Coal

Agriculture
- Cashew nuts
- Cloves
- Coffee
- Corn
- Cotton
- Livestock
- Rice
- Sisal

Manufacturing
- Beer
- Food and beverages
- Textiles
- Furniture/Wood products

Services
- Airport
- Port
- Tourism
- Train station

ABOUT THE ECONOMY

OVERVIEW
Most Tanzanians are employed in agriculture and light industry. Foreign investments in manufacturing, tourism, and mining contribute to real GDP growth. With pickup in industrial production and improvement in the economic infrastructure, Tanzania's vision of becoming a middle-class society may soon materialize.

GROSS DOMESTIC PRODUCT (GDP)
$43.49 billion (2007 estimate)

GDP GROWTH
6.9 percent (2007 estimate)

INFLATION RATE
7 percent (2006 estimate)

LAND USE
Arable land: 4.23 percent
Permanent crops: 1.16 percent
Others: 94.61 percent (2005 estimate)

NATURAL RESOURCES
Hydropower, tin, phosphates, iron ore, coal, diamonds, gemstones, gold, natural gas, and nickel

CURRENCY
Tanzanian Shillings (TZS)
Notes: TSh 500, 1000, 2000, 5000, 10,000
Coins: TSh 5, 10, 20, 50, 100, and 200
1 USD = 1,255 (as of 2007)

AGRICULTURAL PRODUCTS
Coffee, sisal, tea, cotton, pyrethrum, cashew nuts, tobacco, cloves, corn, wheat, cassava, bananas, fruits, vegetables, cattle, sheep, and goats

INDUSTRY
Tourism, agricultural processing, diamond, gold and iron mining, cement, oil refining, textile, wood products, and fertilizer

MAJOR EXPORTS
Gold, coffee, cashew nuts, manufactures, and cotton

MAJOR IMPORTS
Consumer goods, machinery and transportation equipment, industrial raw materials, and crude oil

MAIN TRADE PARTNERS
South Africa, China, Kenya, India, Netherlands, Japan, United Arab Emirates, Germany, and Zambia

POPULATION BELOW POVERTY LINE
36 percent (2002 estimate)

WORKFORCE
19.69 million (2007 estimate)

UNEMPLOYMENT RATE
Not applicable. 80 percent employed in agriculture; 20 percent employed in industry (2007 estimate)

EXTERNAL DEBT
$4.98 billion (2007 estimate)

CULTURAL TANZANIA

Mwanza
Dancing and drumming with the Sukuma, and excellent birding at nearby Rubondo Island National Park.

Serengeti National Park
Magnificent east African wilderness and the annual wild beast migration.

Ngorongoro Crater
Best wildlife and bird-viewing area; the Masai tend their cattle here.

Mount Kilimanjaro
Magnificent sight of Africa's snow-capped mountain on the equator.

Pemba
World-class diving, green landscape, and cultural mystique.

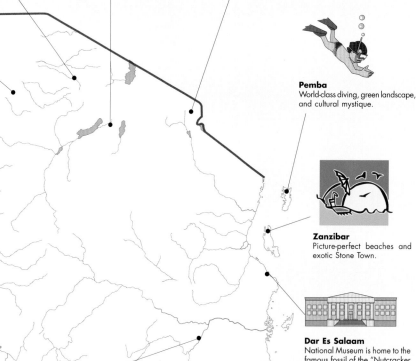

Zanzibar
Picture-perfect beaches and exotic Stone Town.

Dar Es Salaam
National Museum is home to the famous fossil of the "Nutcracker Man" from Olduvai Gorge, and displays from the Shirazi civilization, slave trade, and colonial periods.

Selous Game Reserve
Boat safaris along the Rufiji River and excellent wildlife watching.

ABOUT THE CULTURE

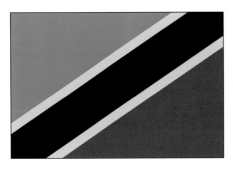

OFFICIAL NAME
United Republic of Tanzania

FLAG DESCRIPTION
Divided diagonally by a yellow-edged black band from the lower hoisting-side corner. The upper triangle (hoisting side) is green and the lower one is blue.

CAPITAL
Dodoma (official capital)
Dar es Salaam (commercial capital)

POPULATION
40.2 million (2008 estimate)

BIRTHRATE
35.12 births per 1,000 Tanzanians (2008 estimate)

DEATH RATE,
12.92 deaths per 1,000 Tanzanians (2008 estimate)

AGE DISTRIBUTION
0–14 years: 43.5 percent
15–64 years: 53.7 percent
65 years and over: 2.8 percent (2008 estimate)

ETHNIC GROUPS
Mainland African (130 tribes): 99 percent
Others (Asian, European, Arab): 1 percent

RELIGIOUS GROUPS
Mainland Christian: 30 percent
Muslim: 35 percent
Indigenous beliefs: 35 percent
Zanzibar Muslims: 99 percent

MAIN LANGUAGES
Kiswahili (Swahili) and English (official), Arabic

LITERACY RATE
69.4 percent (2002 estimate)

IMPORTANT HOLIDAYS
New Year (January 1); Zanzibar Revolution Day (January 12); Moulid el-Nabi (March or April); Union Day (April 26); Workers' Day (May 1); Independence Day (December 9); Christmas (December 25)

LEADERS IN POLITICS
Julius Nyerere—president (1964–85)
Ali Hassan Mwinyi—president (1985–95)
Benjamin Mkapa—president (1995–2005)
Jakaya Kikwete—president (2005–present)

TIME LINE

IN TANZANIA	IN THE WORLD
8000 B.C. • The Khoisan settle in and around Olduvai Gorge.	• **A.D. 600** Height of Mayan civilization
A.D. 750 • Islam arrives on the East African coast. Swahili civilization begins to prosper.	
1300 Kilwa becomes a powerful trade center along the East African coast.	• **1000** The Chinese perfect gunpowder and use it in warfare.
1506 • The Portuguese control the East African coast.	
1530 • Beginning of transatlantic slave trade organized by the Portuguese	• **1558–1603** Reign of Elizabeth I of England
1699 The Omani Arabs oust the Portuguese from Zanzibar.	• **1620** Pilgrims sail the *Mayflower* to America.
1840 • The sultan of Oman sets up court in Zanzibar.	• **1869** The Suez Canal is opened.
1884 • German Colonization Society begins to acquire territory on the mainland of Tanzania.	
1886 • Britain and Germany sign agreement for Germans to set up a sphere of influence over mainland Tanzania, while Britain enjoys a protectorate over Zanzibar.	
1905–6 • An indigenous Maji Maji revolt is suppressed by German troops.	• **1914** World War I begins.
1946 The United Nations converts the British mandate over Tanganyika into a trusteeship.	• **1939** World War II begins.
1954 • Julius Nyerere and Oscar Kambona transform the Tanganyika African Association into the Tanganyika African National Union.	
1961 • Tanganyika becomes independent, with Julius Nyerere as prime minister.	
1962 • Tanganyika becomes a republic, with Nyerere as president.	

IN TANZANIA	IN THE WORLD
1963 Zanzibar becomes independent **1964** The Afro-Shirazi Party overthrows the Sultanate of Zanzibar. Tanganyika and Zanzibar merge to become Tanzania. **1977** The Tanganyika African National Union and Zanzibar's Afro-Shirazi Party merge to become the Party of the Revolution, the only legal political party. **1979** Tanzanian forces invade Uganda, occupying the capital of Kampala, and help oust Ugandan President Idi Amin. **1985** Nyerere retires and is replaced by the president of Zanzibar, Ali Mwinyi. **1992** The constitution is amended to allow multiparty politics. **1995** Benjamin Mkapa is chosen as president in Tanzania's first multiparty election. **1999** Julius Nyerere dies in October. **2000** Benjamin Mkapa is elected for a second term, winning 72 percent of the votes. **2001** Bulyanhulu gold mine opens near Mwanza, making Tanzania Africa's third largest producer of gold. **2005** Political violence in Zanzibar; Jakaya Kikwete wins presidential elections **2008** Central Bank Governor Daudi Ballali is fired after an international audit finds that the bank made improper payments of more than $120 million to local companies.	**1986** Nuclear power disaster at Chernobyl in Ukraine **1997** Hong Kong is returned to China. **2003** The war in Iraq begins. **2004** Indian Ocean earthquake and tsunami

GLOSSARY

Bantu
African tribes originally from the Niger-Congo region that all speak a common group of languages.

bui-bui
Head-covering worn by some Muslim women.

bwana
A term of respect used for men that literally means "father of many sons."

dagaa (**da-GAH**)
Sardinelike fish.

dala dala
Minivans.

gombe sugu
A Tanzanian dance.

habari (**ha-BAR-ree**)
News.

iftar
The first meal a Muslim eats when breaking his or her fast at sunset.

jambo (**YAM-boh**)
Greeting used by Tanzanians.

kahk
Sweet biscuits eaten on Ramadan.

kanzu
An ankle-length robe worn by Muslim men.

karibuni (**ka-ree-BOO-nee**)
Welcome.

Konge
A Tanzanian dance.

konyagi (**kon-YAH-gee**)
Beer made from sugarcane.

lele mama
A Tanzanian dance.

Loibon
Masai prophet.

mangala
A Tanzanian dance.

matatu (**ma-TAH-too**)
A minibus taxi.

Midimu
Makonde harvest celebration.

miombo
Woodlands with only a sparse cover of trees.

moran (**MO-RARN**)
A young Masai warrior.

moruo (**MOR-oo-oo**)
A junior elder among the Masai.

mzee (**m-ZEE**)
A term of respect used by a younger person to an older person.

Ngai
The god of the Masai.

ngoma (**un-GOH-mah**)
Traditional dances.

popobawa
Mythical dwarf with one eye and batlike wings.

rift valleys
Volcanic splits in the Earth's surface.

taarab
Traditional music from Egypt, played with fiddles, flutes, drums and rattles, and singing.

tembo
An alcoholic drink produced from coconuts.

ujamaa (**oo-JAH-mah**)
A state-controlled community village.

wamachinga
Mobile shopkeepers.

FURTHER INFORMATION

BOOKS

Amin, Mohammed, D. C. Willotts, and J. Eames. *The Last of the Maasai.* Cape Town: Struik, 1987.

Briggs, Philip. *Guide to Tanzania.* Bucks, England: Bradt Publications, 2006.

Mercer, Graham, and Javed Jafferji. *Tanzania—African Eden.* Zanzibar: The Gallery Publications, 2001.

Murray, Jocelyn, editor. *Cultural Atlas of Africa.* London: Phaidon Press Ltd, 1981.

Vassanji, M. G. *The Gunny Sack.* Port Moody, Canada: Anchor, 2005.

FILMS

Salkeld, Audrey. *Kilimanjaro: To the Roof of Africa.* National Geographic, 2002

WEBSITES

Central Intelligence Agency World Factbook (select Tanzania from country list) www.cia.gov/cia/publications/factbook/index.html

The Life and Myth of Bi Kidude. (www.asoldasmytongue.net)

The Official Tanzania National Web site (www.tanzania.go.tz)

Recipe Source (www.recipesource.com)

The Tanzanian Development Vision 2025 (www.tanzania.go.tz/vision.htm)

BIBLIOGRAPHY

Barzini, Luigi. *The Europeans*. New York: Simon & Schuster, 1983.
Cameron, Fiona. *We Live in Belgium and Luxembourg*. Sussex, England: Wayland, 1986.
Finke, Jens. *The Rough Guide to Tanzania*. Rough Guides, 2006.
Fitzpatrick, Mary. *Tanzania*. Lonely Planet, 2005.
Lewis, Flora. *Europe*. New York: Simon & Schuster, 1987.
Stevenson, Victor. *Evolution of Western Languages*. New York: Van Nostrand Reinhold, 1990.
Central Intelligence Agency—The World Factbook. www.cia.gov/library/publications/the-world-factbook/geos/lu.html

INDEX

WITHDRAWN